www.wadsworth.com

www.wadsworth.com is the World Wide Web site for Wadsworth and is your direct source to dozens of online resources.

At *www.wadsworth.com* you can find out about supplements, demonstration software, and student resources. You can also send email to many of our authors and preview new publications and exciting new technologies.

www.wadsworth.com
Changing the way the world learns®

Rudiments of Music
for Music Majors
with CD

Rudiments of Music
for Music Majors
with CD

Eileen Soskin

Peabody Institute of Music at Johns Hopkins University

SCHIRMER
CENGAGE Learning™

Australia • Brazil • Japan • Korea • Mexico • Singapore • Spain • United Kingdom • United States

SCHIRMER
CENGAGE Learning™

Rudiments of Music for Music Majors with CD
Eileen Soskin

Publisher/Executive Editor: Clark Baxter

Acquisitions Editor: Clark Baxter

Senior Assistant Editor: Julie Yardley

Editorial Assistant: Anne Gittinger

Technology Project Manager:
  Michelle Vardeman

Marketing Manager: Diane Wenckebach

Marketing Assistant: Rachel Bairstow

Advertising Project Manager: Kelley McAllister

Project Manager, Editorial Production:
  Emily Smith

Print/Media Buyer: Barbara Britton

Permissions Editor: Sarah Harkrader

Production Service:
  Stratford Publishing Services

Copy Editor: Carrie Crompton

Compositor: Stephen Stone

Cover Designer: Laurie Anderson

Cover Image: "Green Haze of Time," by Ann
  Monn, © Corbis Images

For product information and technology assistance, contact us at
Cengage Learning Customer & Sales Support, 1-800-354-9706
For permission to use material from this text or product, submit all requests online at **cengage.com/permissions**
Further permissions questions can be emailed to
permissionrequest@cengage.com

Library of Congress Control Number: 2004101122

ISBN-13: 978-0-534-63828-3
ISBN-10: 0-534-63828-7

Schirmer
25 Thomson Place
Boston, MA 02210-1202
USA

Cengage Learning is a leading provider of customized learning solutions with office locations around the globe, including Singapore, the United Kingdom, Australia, Mexico, Brazil and Japan. Locate your local office at: **international.cengage.com/region**

Cengage Learning products are represented in Canada by Nelson Education, Ltd.

For your course and learning solutions, visit **academic.cengage.com**

Purchase any of our products at your local college store or at our preferred online store **www.ichapters.com**

Printed in the United States of America
6 7 8 9 10 11   13 12 11 10

Contents

Preface

This book is designed specifically for college-level music majors, many of whom are not sufficiently familiar with music rudiments to succeed in a freshman theory course. Three options are available to such students:

1. A remedial music theory course in the freshman year;

2. Intensive study over the summer preceding the freshman year; or

3. Enrollment in freshman theory with discouraging results for student and instructor.

Rudiments of Music for Music Majors offers students an opportunity to work on their own or in a classroom. Each homework assignment includes a suggested time limit. Students are expected to understand and become fluent with the materials presented. Fundamentals should be so well known by every serious musician that they require almost no conscious thought, freeing the artist to perform, think, and feel at the highest level.

Listening to music should be a daily activity performed in conjunction with presentation of materials in this book. Musicians must learn to listen intensely, both thinking about and responding emotionally to sound. The intent listener is rewarded by experiencing and understanding more of the music. All of the topics in this book must be related to listening on a daily basis.

This book includes drills and listening suggestions keyed to the Dover edition of the *Complete String Quartets* by Ludwig van Beethoven, which is recommended to all readers as a supplement to this text. The accompanying CD-ROM offers additional drills to supplement the materials in each chapter.

Acknowledgments

My special thanks to Clark Baxter, Julie Yardley, Nancy Crompton, and Carrie Crompton, my publishers and editors, whose careful work and endless patience made the process a delight. I also wish to express my deep gratitude to my colleagues Tom Benjamin and Stephen Stone, whose suggestions and encouragement have been most valuable. Most of all, I want to acknowledge my debt to my students, all of whom have taught me a great deal as we shared our love of music.

Suggestions for the Reader

Listening

Listen to music every single day—on the radio, on CDs, at concerts and rehearsals. When possible, listen to pieces you do not know well. Choose music from a wide range of styles and genres. All of the topics covered in this text are relevant to how we hear music. You are strongly encouraged to make active listening a lifelong goal, working to stay engaged with all the music you hear. Try to describe every piece of music you hear in the following terms:

melodic patterns
rhythmic patterns
meter
dynamics (using terms listed on page 10 of Chapter 1)
tempo (using terms listed on page 10 of Chapter 1)
instruments (and/or voice types)
language (of a vocal piece)
mode
number of measures per phrase
harmonic rhythm
genre (solo, chamber, choral, operatic, or orchestral)
phrasing
range and register

The more intently you listen to music, the more you will find yourself truly aware of its content. When you listen actively, you hear more and feel more; you are part of every musical performance you hear.

Suggestions

Once you understand the material being presented, be sure to practice repeatedly until you have built up considerable speed. If possible, practice at a piano. This is particularly important when you are working on scales, intervals, and triads. If you are not a pianist, practice scales on your instrument or with your voice, playing or singing while naming the notes. Precision in notation also should be practiced diligently. Notation is an important means of communication for musicians.

It is recommended that you purchase the Dover edition of the Complete String Quartets of Beethoven: Ludwig van Beethoven, *Complete String Quartets*. New York: Dover, 1970 (ISBN 0-486-22361-2). References to this score are made throughout this text and offer ways to understand and reinforce the materials presented while working with great compositions.

CHAPTER ONE   Note Names and Clefs

Our notational system developed in response to the need for visual cues. Musicians communicate through a shared system of notation. One element of this system is the notation of pitch events, which was developed when the demands of an oral tradition became too great for performers.

1.   Letter Names

Western music uses the first seven letters of the alphabet as note names.

A	B	C	D	E	F	G	A
A	G	F	E	D	C	B	A

Drill: Practice saying these seven letter names both forward and backward, starting on each one in turn (begin on A and ascend to A; begin again on A and descend to A; then begin on B and ascend to B; begin again on B and descend to B; and so on). Be sure to keep a steady beat throughout each exercise; push yourself to go faster and faster.

Drill: Practice speaking the letter names, skipping every other one, going up until you reach the starting letter name and then going backwards. Start on each of the seven letter names (begin on A and ascend to A [A C E G B D F A]; begin again on A and descend to A [A F D B G E C A]; then begin on B and ascend to B; begin again on B and descend to B; and so on). Be sure to keep a steady beat throughout each exercise; push yourself to go faster and faster.

These seven letter names are the white notes of the modern piano.

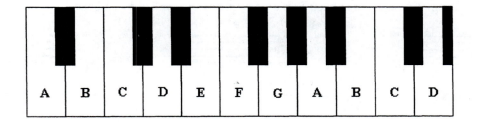

2.   Clefs

The music staff in use today has five lines enclosing four spaces:

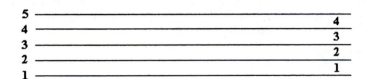

A clef is a sign that indicates the particular location of the seven letter names. The two most common clefs are the treble clef and the bass clef.

treble clef (G-clef)

bass clef (F-clef)

The treble clef generally indicates higher pitches than the bass clef, but the clefs share many pitches.

Other clefs in use today include C-clefs and another F-clef. The most common of these is the alto clef, read by violas most of the time.

The other C-clefs are the soprano, mezzo-soprano, and tenor clefs. The soprano and mezzo-soprano clefs are rarely encountered. The tenor clef is frequently used by both violoncelli and trombones.

soprano clef   mezzo-soprano clef   tenor clef

The other F-clef is the baritone clef. It is rarely used.

Drill: Practice writing treble, bass, and alto clef signs on the staves below until your manuscript is both legible and quick.

3.   Treble Clef

Read aloud the pitches written on the treble clef below, forward and backward.

D   E   F   G   A   B   C   D   E   F   G   F   E   D   C   B   A   G   F   E   D

Read aloud the pitches written on the treble staff below, up and down (reading by thirds).

Ledger lines are short, unbroken lines that are added above and below any staff to extend its range.

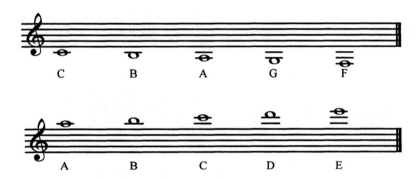

Drill: Say letter names aloud, quickly, for the Violin I part (top line) of Beethoven's String Quartet Op. 59, No. 3, fourth movement (last two lines of page 18 (196) and the first line of page (197) 19).*

Homework Assignments #1 and #2, pp. 13-14

---

* Page references are to the Dover edition of the *Complete String Quartets* by Ludwig van Beethoven, recommended as a supplement to this text.

4.   Accidentals

Any letter name may be altered by an accidental sign. Accidentals alter a pitch, making it sound higher or lower.
There are five common accidentals: sharp, flat, natural, double sharp, and double flat. In written notation,
accidentals *precede* the pitch they alter. In speech, accidentals *follow* the pitch they alter.

sharp	♯	raises pitch by a half step
flat	♭	lowers pitch by a half step
natural	♮	erases a previous accidental or raises a flatted pitch by a half step or lowers a sharped pitch by a half step
double sharp	✕	raises pitch by a whole step
double flat	♭♭	lowers pitch by a whole step

Drill: Practice writing each accidental sign until yours look like the printed ones. Your manuscript
writing should always be as clear as possible. Music manuscript is a means of communicating
with other musicians.

Accidentals alter pitches for an entire measure.

A   G♯   A   E   A   G♯   A

An accidental is canceled by a bar line, but the cancellation is often specified in the following measure. This is a
courtesy accidental: it is not required (because the bar line cancels the G♯ of the previous measure), but it is
usually included as a reminder to the musician.

A   G♯   A   E   A   B   C   B   A   G♮   F   E   A

5

Accidentals apply only to the specific pitch that they alter, not to a pitch an octave away.

A   G♯   A   E   A   A   G♮   F

Drill: Continuing on page (197) 19 of the Beethoven, read the Violin I part from the second staff to the bottom of the page, saying aloud all of the note names, including the accidentals.

5.   Bass Clef

Read aloud the pitches written on the bass clef below, forward and backward.

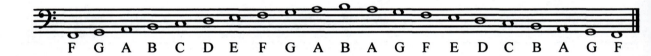

F   G   A   B   C   D   E   F   G   A   B   A   G   F   E   D   C   B   A   G   F

Read aloud the pitches written on the bass staff below, forward and backward (reading by thirds).

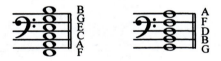

Ledger lines may be added above and below the bass clef to extend its range.

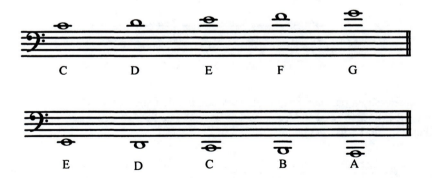

C   D   E   F   G

E   D   C   B   A

Drill: Beginning on the third staff of page 18 (196), read aloud the violoncello line (the bottom line) through the first staff of (197) 19, saying aloud all of the note names, including the accidentals.

Homework Assignments #3, #4, #5, and #6, pp. 15-18

6.   Alto Clef

The third line of the alto clef is middle C on the piano.

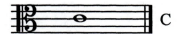

Read aloud the pitches written on the alto clef below, forward and backward.

E   F   G   A   B   C   D   E   F   G   A   G   F   E   D   C   B   A   G   F   E

Read aloud the pitches written on the alto clef below, forward and backward (reading by thirds).

Ledger lines may be added above and below the alto clef to extend its range.

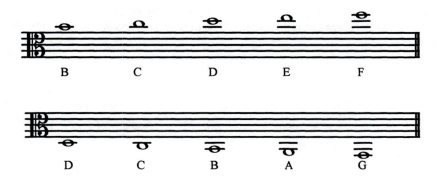

B   C   D   E   F

D   C   B   A   G

Drill: Beginning on page 18 (196), read the viola line (in alto clef) through the first staff of (197) 19, saying aloud all of the note names, including the accidentals.

Homework Assignments #7, #8, #9, and #10, pp. 19-22

7.   The Great Staff

The great staff is created by bracketing treble and bass clefs together. Most piano music is written on the great staff. A system for identifying registers is shown below. Every C begins a new octave.

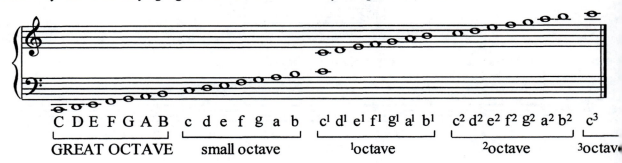

C D E F G A B   c d e f g a b   c¹ d¹ e¹ f¹ g¹ a¹ b¹   c² d² e² f² g² a² b²   c³

$$C \ D \ E \ F \ G \ A \ B \quad c \ d \ e \ f \ g \ a \ b \quad c^1 \ d^1 \ e^1 \ f^1 \ g^1 \ a^1 \ b^1 \quad c^2 \ d^2 \ e^2 \ f^2 \ g^2 \ a^2 \ b^2 \quad c^3$$

GREAT OCTAVE   small octave   ¹octave   ²octave   ³octave

Drill: Cover the identifying notations below the great staff with your hand. Identify randomly picked pitches by letter name *and* octave location.

Homework Assignment #11, p. 23

Double bars may signify the end of a piece of music. Use beginning brackets and closing double bar lines when notating music on the great staff (see example above). Single staves also require closing bar lines. Single staves *do not require* beginning bar lines.

correct   incorrect

Drill: Add the appropriate bar lines to the following examples.

Great Staff:

Single staff:

8

8.   Enharmonic Equivalents

There are only twelve notes in a single octave on the modern piano; however, there are at least two or three possible note names for each note. Enharmonic equivalents are the different names for notes that sound the same.

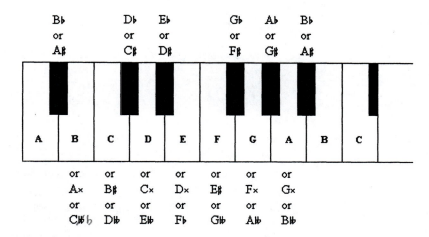

Drill: Name all of the possible names (using sharps, flats, double sharps, and double flats) for the pitches A, B, C, D, E, F, and G.

Drill: Name all of the possible names (using flats, double sharps, and double flats) for the pitches A#, B#, C#, D#, E#, F#, and G#.

Drill: Name all of the possible names (using sharps, double sharps, and double flats) for the pitches Ab, Bb, Cb, Db, Eb, Fb, and Gb.

Homework Assignment #12, p. 24

9.   Dynamics

Dynamics are performance instructions concerning volume given by composers and editors. They are often in Italian, especially in music of the past, as Italian was considered the international language of music. The most common dynamic markings in Western music are given below.

Abbreviation	Italian Term	Definition
ppp	*pianississimo*	very, very soft
pp	*pianissimo*	very soft
p	*piano*	soft
mp	*mezzo piano*	medium soft
mf	*mezzo forte*	medium loud
f	*forte*	loud
ff	*fortissimo*	very loud
fff	*fortississimo*	very, very loud
sfz	*sforzando*	sudden accent
sub.	*subito*	sudden dynamic change
<	*crescendo*	get louder gradually
>	*decrescendo*	get softer gradually
dim.	*diminuendo*	get softer gradually

Drill: Cover everything except the column of abbreviations and, first in order and then randomly, say the Italian name and definition for each term out loud.

10.   Tempo Markings

Tempo markings are performance instructions regarding speed. They are usually given in Italian at the beginning of a composition. They are relative terms, open to interpretation by the performer, unless modified by specific metronome markings. The following ranges of metronome markings are approximate.

Italian Tempo Marking	Metronome Marking	Definition
Prestissimo	200-208	Very, very fast
Vivace, Presto	168-200	Very fast
Allegro	120-168	Fast
Moderato	108-120	Medium
Andante	76-108	Medium
Adagio	65-76	Slow
Larghetto	55-65	Very slow
Largo, Grave	40-60	Very, very slow

Drill: Cover everything except the column on the left and, first in order and then randomly, say the approximate metronome markings and give the definition for each term.

Other Common Terms	Definitions
ma non troppo	not too much
con moto	with motion
ritard	slow down
rallentando	slow down
accelerando	speed up
molto	more
meno mosso	a bit less
poco a poco	little by little
sempre	always

Drill: Cover the column on the right and, first in order and then randomly, say each term and give its definition.

PRACTICE QUIZ ON CHAPTER ONE, p. 25

Name: Chris H.

Time limit: 3 minutes

Identify the following notes by letter name.

Example: Given: Answer:

   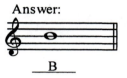

_____   B

1. F⁴ 2. G⁵ 3. D⁴ 4. C⁵ 5. G⁴ 6. E⁵

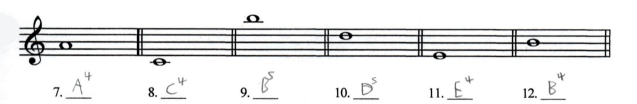

7. A⁴ 8. C⁴ 9. B⁵ 10. D⁵ 11. E⁴ 12. B⁴

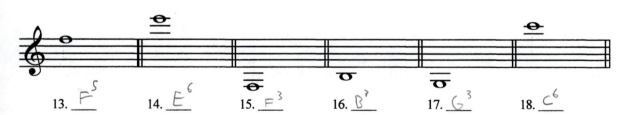

13. F⁵ 14. E⁶ 15. F³ 16. B³ 17. G³ 18. C⁶

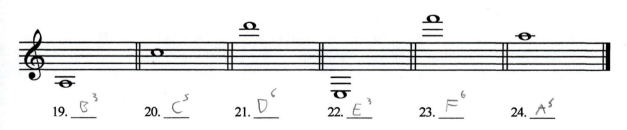

19. B³ 20. C⁵ 21. D⁶ 22. E³ 23. F⁶ 24. A⁵

Answers on page 27

Name: ___Chris H.___   Time limit: 10 minutes

Write the requested notes in as many places as they occur on the treble clef. Use no more than three ledger lines. **Use only whole notes.**

Example: Given: G   Answer:

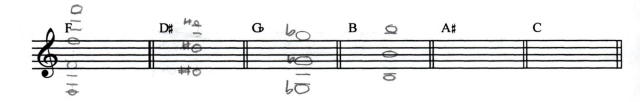

Answers on page 28

Name: _____

Time limit: 3 minutes

Identify the following notes by letter name.

Example: Given: Answer:

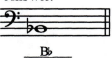

_____   __Bb__

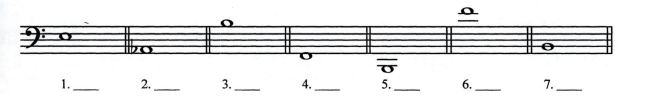

1. ___   2. ___   3. ___   4. ___   5. ___   6. ___   7. ___

8. ___   9. ___   10. ___   11. ___   12. ___   13. ___   14. ___

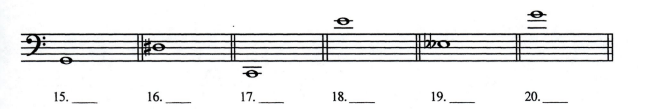

15. ___   16. ___   17. ___   18. ___   19. ___   20. ___

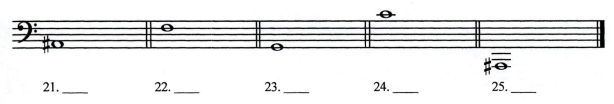

21. ___   22. ___   23. ___   24. ___   25. ___

Answers on page 29

Name: _____   Time limit: 10 minutes

Write the requested notes in as many places as they occur on the bass clef. Use no more than three ledger lines. **Use only whole notes**.

Example: Given: G   Answer:
                                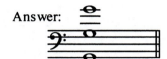

Cb   G#   Ab   E   B#   Fb

A   Db   F   D#   Gb   B

A#   C   Eb   Cb   D   G#

Bb   F#   C#   A   G   E#

Answers on page 30

16

Name: _____

Identify the following notes by letter name.

Example: Given: Answer:

   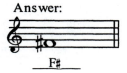

_____   _____F#_____

1. ____   2. ____   3. ____   4. ____   5. ____   6. ____   7. ____

8. ____   9. ____   10. ____   11. ____   12. ____   13. ____

14. ____   15. ____   16. ____   17. ____   18. ____   19. ____

20. ____   21. ____   22. ____   23. ____   24. ____   25. ____

Answers on page 31

17

Name:_____

Write the requested notes in as many places as they occur on the given clef. Use no more than three ledger lines. **Use only whole notes**.

Example: Given: G   Answer:

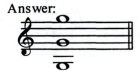

Answers on page 32

Name: _____

Time limit: 6 minutes

Identify the following notes by letter name.

Example: Given: Answer:

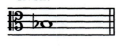

____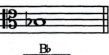

B♭

1. ____   2. ____   3. ____   4. ____   5. ____   6. ____   7. ____

8. ____   9. ____   10. ____   11. ____   12. ____   13. ____

14. ____   15. ____   16. ____   17. ____   18. ____   19. ____

20. ____   21. ____   22. ____   23. ____   24. ____   25. ____

Answers on page 33

Name: _____   Time limit: 10 minutes

Write the requested notes in as many places as they occur on the alto clef. Use no more than three ledger lines. **Use only whole notes**.

Example: Given: G   Answer:

A   C   B♭   F   D♭   B   G♭

D   A♯   G   C♯   E   D♯

B♭   F♯   A♭   G♭   D   G♯

Answers on page 34

20

Name: _____

Time limit: 10 minutes

Identify the following notes by letter name.

Example: Given: Answer:

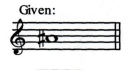   

_____   __A#__

1. ____   2. ____   3. ____   4. ____   5. ____   6. ____

7. ____   8. ____   9. ____   10. ____   11. ____   12. ____

13. ____   14. ____   15. ____   16. ____   17. ____   18. ____

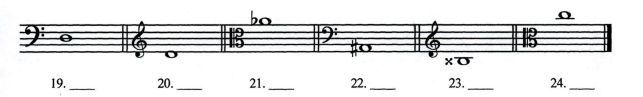

19. ____   20. ____   21. ____   22. ____   23. ____   24. ____

Answers on page 35

Name: _____   Time limit: 10 minutes

Identify the following notes by letter name.

Example: Given: Answer:

   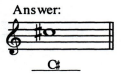

_____   _____ C#

1. ____   2. ____   3. ____   4. ____   5. ____   6. ____

7. ____   8. ____   9. ____   10. ____   11. ____   12. ____

13. ____   14. ____   15. ____   16. ____   17. ____   18. ____

19. ____   20. ____   21. ____   22. ____   23. ____   24. ____

Answers on page 36

Name: _____   Time limit: 10 minutes

Identify the following notes by letter name and octave location.

Example: Given: Answer:

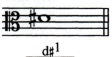

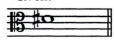

____   ____ d#^{1}

1. ___   2. ___   3. ___   4. ___   5. ___   6. ___

7. ___   8. ___   9. ___   10. ___   11. ___   12. ___

13. ___   14. ___   15. ___   16. ___   17. ___   18. ___

19. ___   20. ___   21. ___   22. ___   23. ___   24. ___

Answers on page 37

23

Name: _____   Time limit: 5 minutes

Write **two** enharmonic equivalents for each given note. You may use naturals, sharps, flats, double sharps, and/or double flats, as needed.

Example:

A#   _____   _____   A#   B♭   C♭

D#   1. ____   2. ____   C   3. ____   4. ____

G   5. ____   6. ____   A×   7. ____   8. ____

F#   9. ____   10. ____   B   11. ____   12. ____

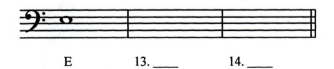

E   13. ____   14. ____

Answers on page 38

24

Name: _____

1. Identify the following notes by letter name and octave location.

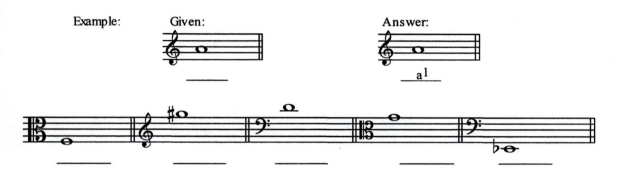

2. Write the requested notes in as many places as they occur in the given clef. Use no more than three ledger lines. **Use only whole notes**.

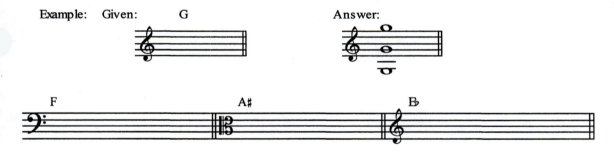

3. Write **two** enharmonic equivalents for each given note, and the letter name of each. You may use naturals, sharps, flats, double sharps, and/or double flats, as needed.

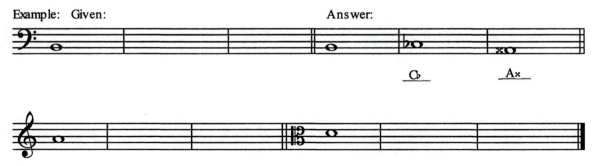

Answers on page 39

Identify the following notes by letter name.

Example: Given: Answer:

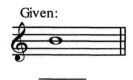   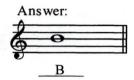

_____   __B__

1. _F_   2. _G_   3. _D_   4. _C_   5. _G_   6. _E_

7. _A_   8. _C_   9. _B_   10. _D_   11. _E_   12. _B_

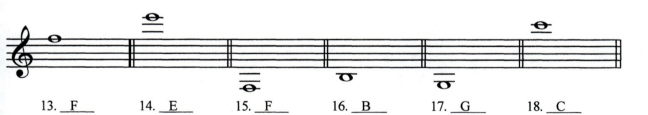

13. _F_   14. _E_   15. _F_   16. _B_   17. _G_   18. _C_

19. _A_   20. _C_   21. _D_   22. _E_   23. _F_   24. _A_

Write the requested notes in as many places as they occur on the treble clef. Use no more than
three ledger lines. **Use only whole notes**.

Example: Given: G

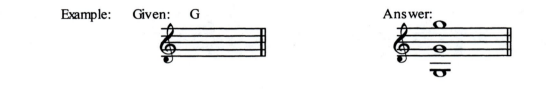

Answer:

Identify the following notes by letter name.

Example: Given: Answer:

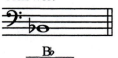

        _____   B♭

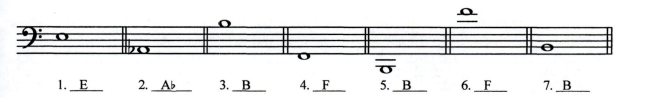

1. _E_   2. _A♭_   3. _B_   4. _F_   5. _B_   6. _F_   7. _B_

8. _G_   9. _D_   10. _A×_   11. _E♯_   12. _C_   13. _D×_   14. _F_

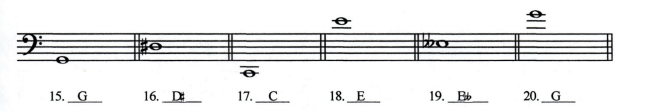

15. _G_   16. _D♯_   17. _C_   18. _E_   19. _E♭_   20. _G_

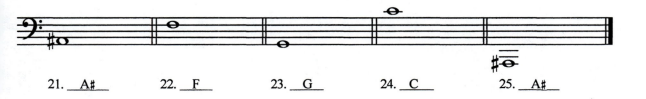

21. _A♯_   22. _F_   23. _G_   24. _C_   25. _A♯_

29

Write the requested notes in as many places as they occur on the bass clef. Use no more than three ledger lines. **Use only whole notes**.

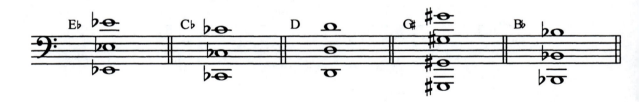

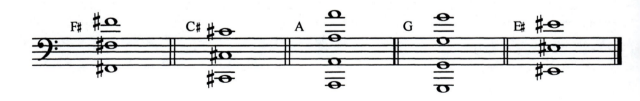

Identify the following notes by letter name.

Example: Given: 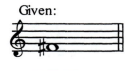   Answer: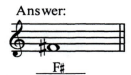

                _____   F#

1. C   2. F#   3. B   4. Ab   5. F#   6. Gb   7. Dx

8. G   9. Cbb   10. Cx   11. G   12. E   13. A

14. A#   15. Bb   16. E#   17. Bbb   18. F   19. A

20. G#   21. D   22. Bb   23. E   24. Gb   25. Gx

Write the requested notes in as many places as they occur on the given clef. Use no more than three ledger lines. **Use only whole notes**.

Identify the following notes by letter name.

Example: Given: Answer:

                    _____   ___Bb___

1. __D__   2. __G#__   3. __F__   4. __B__   5. __Bb__   6. __Gx__   7. __A__

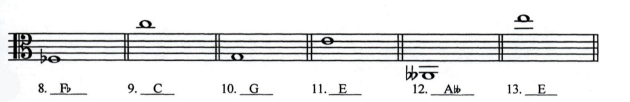

8. __Fb__   9. __C__   10. __G__   11. __E__   12. __Abb__   13. __E__

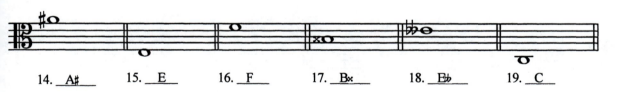

14. __A#__   15. __E__   16. __F__   17. __Bx__   18. __Ebb__   19. __C__

20. __A__   21. __B#__   22. __G__   23. __C#__   24. __Bb__   25. __G#__

Write the requested notes in as many places as they occur on the alto clef. Use no more than three ledger lines. **Use only whole notes**.

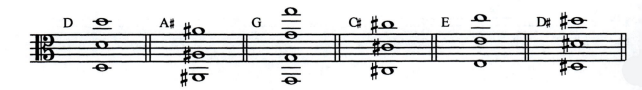

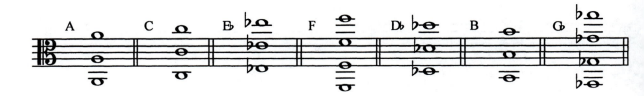

Identify the following notes by letter name.

Example: Given: Answer:

   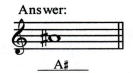

_____   __A#__

1. __C__   2. __A__   3. __C__   4. __Gb__   5. __F__   6. __E__

7. __G#__   8. __D__   9. __A#__   10. __E__   11. __Bb__   12. __A__

13. __Cb__   14. __G__   15. __C__   16. __D__   17. __A__   18. __G__

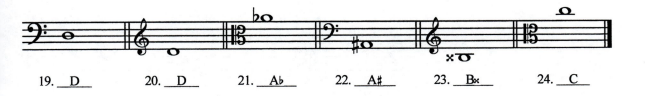

19. __D__   20. __D__   21. __Ab__   22. __A#__   23. __Bx__   24. __C__

Identify the following notes by letter name.

Example: Given: Answer:

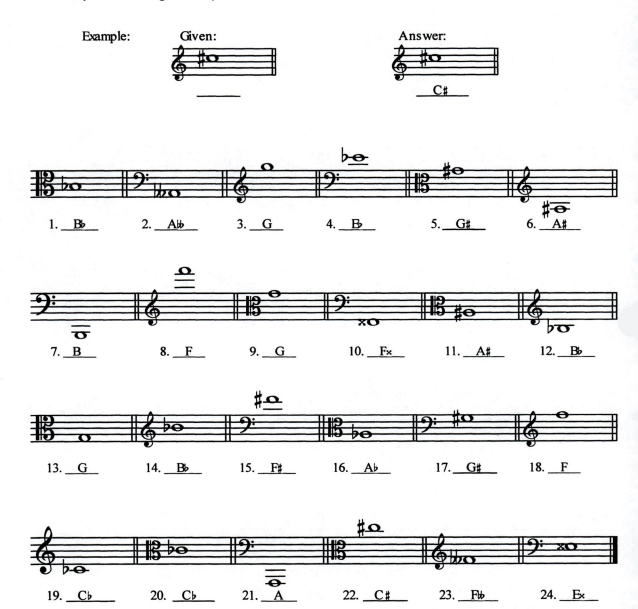

_____   C#

1. __B♭__   2. __A♭♭__   3. __G__   4. __B♭__   5. __G#__   6. __A#__

7. __B__   8. __F__   9. __G__   10. __F✕__   11. __A#__   12. __B♭__

13. __G__   14. __B♭__   15. __F#__   16. __A♭__   17. __G#__   18. __F__

19. __C♭__   20. __C♭__   21. __A__   22. __C#__   23. __F♭♭__   24. __E✕__

Identify the following notes by letter name and octave location.

Example:　　　Given:　　　　　　　　Answer:

d♯¹

1. e♭² 　　 2. A 　　 3. f♯¹ 　　 4. b♭ 　　 5. c³ 　　 6. f¹

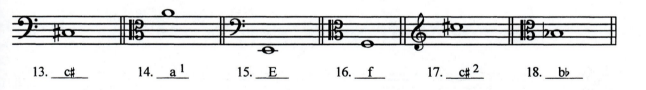

7. g 　　 8. a¹ 　　 9. b♭ 　　 10. b 　　 11. e♭¹ 　　 12. g²

13. c♯ 　　 14. a¹ 　　 15. E 　　 16. f 　　 17. c♯² 　　 18. b♭

19. a♭² 　　 20. c♭ 　　 21. e 　　 22. b♭¹ 　　 23. D 　　 24. d¹

Write **two** enharmonic equivalents for each given note. You may use naturals, sharps, flats, double sharps, and/or double flats, as needed.

Example:

Given: Answer:

A#   _____   _____   A#   Bb   Cb

D#   1. _Bb_   2. _Fbb_   C   3. _B#_   4. _Dbb_

G   5. _Abb_   6. _Fx_   Ax   7. _B_   8. _Cb_

F#   9. _Gb_   10. _Ex_   B   11. _Cb_   12. _Ax_

E   13. _Fb_   14. _Dx_

1. Identify the following notes by letter name and octave location.

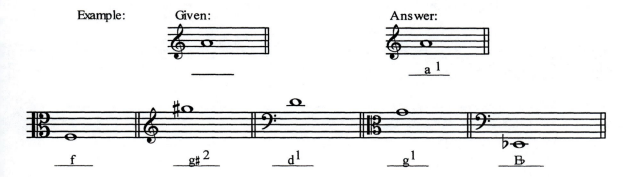

2. Write the requested notes in as many places as they occur in the given clef. Use no more than
   three ledger lines. **Use only whole notes**.

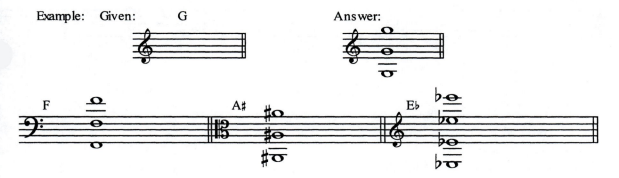

3. Write **two** enharmonic equivalents for each given note, and the letter name of each. You may
   use naturals, sharps, flats, double sharps, and/or double flats, as needed.

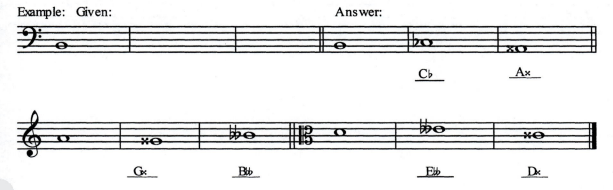

1. Identify the following notes by letter name and octave location. (2 points each; 10 points total)

_____   _____   _____   _____   _____   _____

2. Write the requested notes in as many places as they occur in the given clef. Use **no more than three** ledger lines. Use only whole notes. (3 points each; 9 points total)

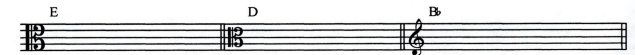

3. Write **two** enharmonic equivalents for each given note, and the letter name of each enharmonic equivalent. You may use naturals, sharps, flats, double sharps, and/or double flats, as needed. (2 points each; 8 points total)

_____   _____   _____   _____

Rhythm and Meter

Another element in the notational system developed by musicians concerns durations, indications to performers of how long a pitch or silence should be.

1.   Notation of Rhythm

Musical durations are primarily determined by tempo, although, in general, smaller note values are faster than larger note values. All note values are relative to each other.

Rhythmic notation includes systems for sounds (pitches) and silences (rests). The symbols in the chart below begin with relatively long durations and progress to relatively short durations. Every duration is half again as long as the preceding duration. (If a *breve* in a given tempo is held for four seconds, a *whole note* in the same tempo is held for two seconds.) Every duration is twice as long as the following duration. (If a *half note* in a given tempo is held for one second, a *whole note* is held for two seconds.)

Note Value	Proper Name	Rest Symbol	Proper Name
	breve		double whole rest
	whole note		whole rest
	half note		half rest
	quarter note		quarter rest
	eighth note		eighth rest
	sixteenth note		sixteenth rest
	thirty-second note		thirty-second rest
	sixty-fourth note		sixty-fourth rest

Drill: Cover the *proper name* categories in the chart above and randomly choose and name symbols for notes and rests.

All notes are written with elliptical shapes called note heads. All notes use stems, except for the breve and whole note. Stems are straight lines about three spaces in length.

> Drill: Practice writing white and black note-heads without stems on the following staff. When writing black note-heads, do not make circles and fill them in. This gives the look of lollipops, not pitches.

Homework Assignments #1 and #2, pp. 51-53

In all single-line music, notes above the third line of the staff have stems on their left side that go down.

In all single-line music, notes below the third line of the staff have stems on their right side that go up.

Pitches on the third line of the staff may have a stem on either side, depending on their context: look at the surrounding pitches and make the choice that gives the greatest consistency.

All notes shorter than a quarter note have flags when written individually. All flags are on the right-hand side of the stem. Groups of notes with flags are usually beamed together.

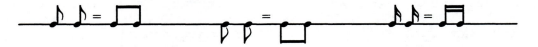

> Drill: Add the appropriate number of flags to the following notes.

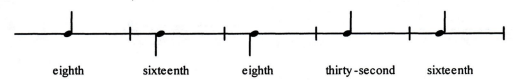

eighth   sixteenth   eighth   thirty-second   sixteenth

Homework Assignments #3, #4, and #5, pp. 54-56

The durations (pitches and rests) that have already been introduced are systematically ordered so that each is twice as long or twice as short as its adjacent notation. Within a given tempo, a whole note is twice as long as a half note; a half note is half as long as a whole note. Two quarter notes are always as long as one half note within a single tempo.

Drill: Referring to the chart on page 41, choose durations at random and describe them in terms of the preceding and following durations. For example: *quarter note*: There are two quarter notes in a half note; there are two eighth notes in a quarter note.

Rhythmic notation may be altered by the addition of a dot that increases the value by half of the note or rest it modifies.

Drill: Referring to the chart on page 41, choose durations and rests at random and describe their length as affected by the addition of a dot. (For example: *quarter note*: There are two eighth notes in a quarter note; therefore, a *dotted quarter note* has a duration of three eighth notes.)

Groupings that are not simple divisions into half (e.g., a half note divides into two quarter notes; a quarter note divides into two eighth notes) are called artificial groupings and are written with brackets or slurs above or below the affected durations. These subdivisions occupy the same duration as natural groupings (for example, an eighth note triplet has the same duration as two eighth notes: that is, a quarter-note duration).

Artificial Grouping	Notation	Equivalent Durational Value
triplet		
quintuplet		
sextuplet		

Homework Assignments #6 and #7, pp. 57-58

2.   Meter

Rhythms are frequently grouped into regular patterns of accented and unaccented beats. When a pattern repeats, each occurrence is called a measure. A measure is a unit containing a specific number of beats. A measure has a specific duration determined by the tempo.

Measures are separated by bar lines which are artificial reminders of the meter. Meter specifies the regular rhythmic patterns and their contents, and is written with two numbers (*never* as a fraction).

$\begin{array}{rcl} x & = & \text{number of beats per unit} \\ y & = & \text{beat unit} \end{array}$

$\begin{array}{rcl} 2 & = & \text{2 beats per measure} \\ 4 & = & \text{quarter note is the beat} \end{array}$ (2 ♩ per measure)

$\begin{array}{rcl} 3 & = & \text{3 beats per measure} \\ 4 & = & \text{quarter note is the beat} \end{array}$ (3 ♩ per measure)

$\begin{array}{rcl} 4 & = & \text{4 beats per measure} \\ 4 & = & \text{quarter note is the beat} \end{array}$ (4 ♩ per measure)

$\begin{array}{rcl} 2 & = & \text{2 beats per measure} \\ 2 & = & \text{half note is the beat} \end{array}$ (2 ♩ per measure)

$\begin{array}{rcl} 3 & = & \text{3 beats per measure} \\ 2 & = & \text{half note is the beat} \end{array}$ (3 ♩ per measure)

$\begin{array}{rcl} 2 & = & \text{2 beats per measure} \\ 8 & = & \text{eighth note is the beat} \end{array}$ (2 ♪ per measure)

$\begin{array}{rcl} 3 & = & \text{3 beats per measure} \\ 8 & = & \text{eighth note is the beat} \end{array}$ (3 ♪ per measure)

$\begin{array}{rcl} 4 & = & \text{4 beats per measure} \\ 8 & = & \text{eighth note is the beat} \end{array}$ (4 ♪ per measure)

Tempo affects our perception of meter. In $\frac{3}{4}$, at a moderate tempo, we hear three beats per measure; at a very slow tempo, we may hear six beats per measure.

Drill: Listen to the opening of Beethoven's String Quartet Op. 18, No. 1, third movement, then look at the score (page (13) 13). Due to the very fast tempo, the three quarter notes per measure are more easily heard as one beat per measure with a triple subdivision. Listen to the opening of Beethoven's String Quartet Op. 59, No. 3, third movement, then look at the score (page 14 (192)). Due to the moderate tempo, the three quarter notes per measure are easily heard as three beats per measure. Listen to the opening of Beethoven's String Quartet Op. 130, first

45

movement, then look at the score. Due to the slow tempo and the subdivision into eighth notes, the three quarter notes per measure are easily heard as six beats per measure.

<u>Drill</u>: Look at the opening of Beethoven's String Quartet Op. 74, third movement (page (12) 12). Will this sound like one beat per measure, three beats per measure, or six beats per measure? Listen to the recording to check your answer.

In traditional Western music, meters are classified as either simple or compound. All simple meters sound with duple backgrounds. For example, in $\frac{3}{4}$, there are three beats per measure (three quarter notes) that most often are heard to subdivide into background groupings of three pairs of eighth notes. Thus the background groupings are of eighth notes; the foreground groupings are of quarter notes.

All compound meters sound with triple backgrounds. For example, in $\frac{6}{8}$, there are six eighth notes per measure, but they are grouped into two units, each containing three eighth notes. Thus, the background groupings are of eighth notes; the foreground groupings are of dotted quarter notes. The beat in $\frac{6}{8}$ is actually a dotted quarter note. The beat in compound meters is always a dotted note.

All compound meters look and sound as if their divisions are triplets without using any special triplet notation.

Homework Assignment #8, pp. 59-60

Meters usually designate two, three, or four beats per measure and are called duple meter, triple meter, and quadruple meter, respectively.

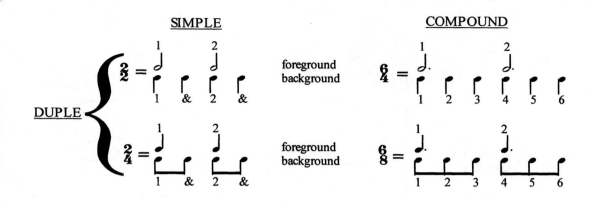

All meters have relatively strong and weak beats, as shown below. These are natural accents that may be subverted by the addition of marked accents. In all meters, the downbeat (the first beat of the measure) is normally accented relative to the other beats.

Meter	Natural Accents	Example
duple meters ╱ = strong beat* U = weak beat*	╱ U 1 2	$\frac{2}{4}$ = (musical notation)
triple meters	╱ U U 1 2 3	$\frac{9}{8}$ = (musical notation)
quadruple meters	╱ U ╱ U 1 2 3 4	$\frac{4}{2}$ = (musical notation)

* Beats are relatively strong or weak. In $\frac{4}{4}$, beat 1 is strong relative to beat 2, but if beat 1 is subdivided into eighth notes, the first eighth note is strong relative to the second one.

Two conventions in metrical notation are:

C means $\frac{4}{4}$ and is called common time

¢ means $\frac{2}{2}$ and is called cut time

Drill: Review the table of meters by speaking aloud the numbers for the foreground and background subdivisions for each meter. For example, for $\frac{2}{4}$, say: *quarter-quarter, 1, 2; eighth-eighth-eighth-eighth, 1 and 2 and.* Be sure to do this with a steady and evenly divided beat.

Drill: Look at the beginning of each movement of Beethoven's String Quartet Op. 18, No. 5 (pages (83) 1, 6 (88), 18 (90), and (95) 13). Using the syllable *tah*, read aloud the first four measures the Violin I and Violoncello lines for each movement. Then read them using background beats (2, 3, 4, or 6) and foreground beats (duple, triple, or quadruple).

Be sure your spoken accents match the natural strong and weak accents unless the music indicates otherwise. For example, look at Op. 18, No. 4, first movement ((65) 1): after saying aloud both Violin I and Violoncello lines for four measures (using the syllable *tah*), say the background beats in tempo: 1 and 2 and 3 and 4; then say the foreground beats: 1, 2, 3, 4.

Homework Assignment #9, pp. 61-62

To identify meter when listening to music, identify strong and weak beats and listen for patterns of long and short durations, keeping in mind the natural accent on the downbeat of each measure. It is critical to concentrate on hearing downbeats. The downbeat will not always be the first durational event in a piece of music. Any durational event preceding the first downbeat is called a pickup, or anacrusis, and is weak relative to the downbeat. Pickup durations are subtracted from the final complete measure of a composition or exercise (in $\frac{4}{4}$, a pickup of one beat necessitates a last measure of only three beats).

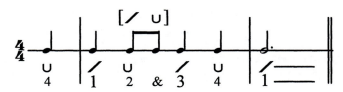

Drill: Listen to the beginning of each movement of Beethoven's String Quartet Op. 59, No. 1. Try to figure out the meter of each movement and, if possible, write down several possibilities for each movement, underlining the one you think most likely. Then look at the score to verify your answers, looking closely at written patterns and accents. Listen to the music again while looking at the score, concentrating on the ways in which Beethoven announces and supports the meter at the beginning of each movement. (See pages (121) 1, (131) 11, (141) 21, and (147) 27.)

You should be able to determine the meter of an unbarred piece of music by looking at durational patterns and recognizing natural accents. For example, what is the meter of the following example?

It is impossible to tell if this example is in $\frac{2}{4}$ or $\frac{4}{4}$ or $\frac{2}{2}$. However, you can tell that it is a simple meter, not a compound one, because there are no groups of three (there are *two* half notes and *four* quarter notes).

It is not possible to tell if there is a half note pickup or if the first note is the downbeat. The following are possible (correct) interpretations of this example:

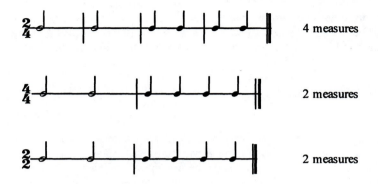

4 measures

2 measures

2 measures

What is the meter of the following example?

You can tell this is a compound meter because there are groupings of three (the dotted quarter subdivides into *three* eighth notes; there is a group of *three* even eighth notes). The following are possible correct interpretations of this example:

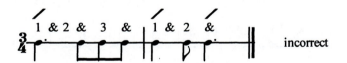

2 measures

4 measures

If you tried to interpret this meter in $\frac{3}{4}$, it would be possible but unlikely up until the last event, at which point $\frac{3}{4}$ is an impossible choice because it accents the second half of the second beat.

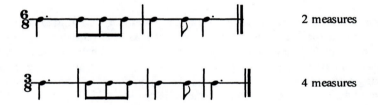

incorrect

Homework Assignment #10, p. 63

PRACTICE QUIZ ON CHAPTER TWO, pp. 64-65

Name: _____   Time limit: 10 minutes

In the space provided, draw two of the pitched and unpitched duration symbols given below.
Label each symbol with its correct name.

Example: Given: Answer:

                                                                  eighth rest

_____   _____

_____   _____

_____   _____

HOMEWORK ASSIGNMENT #1
(continued)

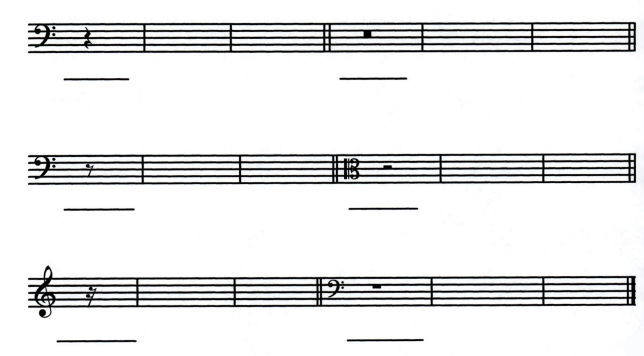

Answers on pages 67-68

Name: _____

Time limit: 5 minutes

Name the following symbols.

Example: Given: Answer: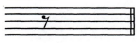

_____   _eighth rest_

Answers on page 69

53

Name: _____

Write the requested symbols in the given clefs. Be careful to put stems and flags on in the right direction.

a¹
quarter note

b
half note

f¹
eighth note

half rest

sixteenth rest

breve rest

g²
quarter note

whole rest

d
quarter note

f♯²
eighth note

b♭
sixteenth note

quarter rest

c¹
sixteenth note

a
eighth note

quarter rest

f♯²
whole note

half rest

F
sixteenth note

a♭¹
eighth note

e¹
half note

D
whole note

b²
half note

a¹
eighth note

b
half note

Answers on page 7

Put stems on the following quarter notes. Choose stem direction **carefully** for the third-line notes,
looking at the surrounding notes.

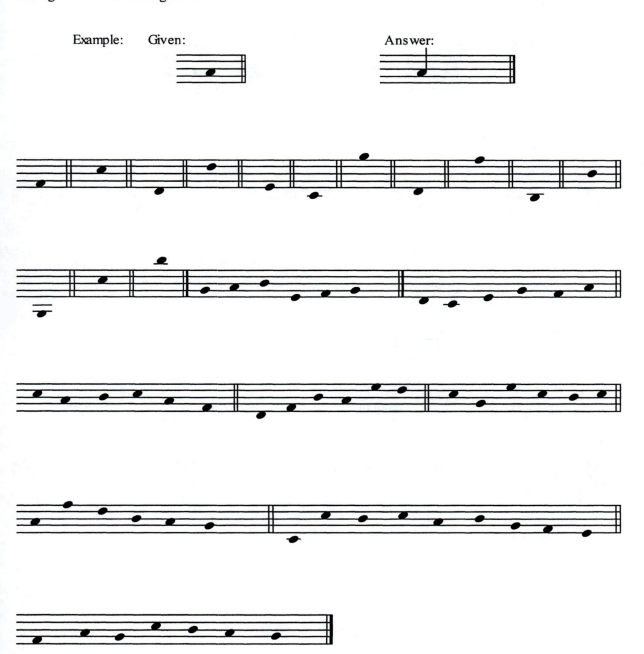

Answers on page 71

Name: _____

Draw the requested note, stem, and flag, as appropriate, in the following examples.

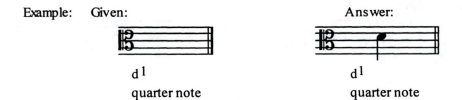

Example: Given: Answer:

d¹
quarter note

d¹
quarter note

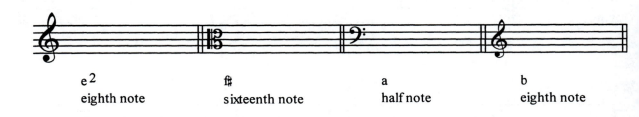

e²   f♯   a   b
eighth note   sixteenth note   half note   eighth note

e♭¹   d¹   g²   e
quarter note   eighth note   sixteenth note   eighth note

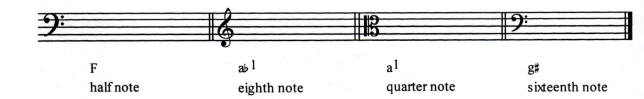

F   a♭¹   a¹   g♯
half note   eighth note   quarter note   sixteenth note

Answers on page 72

Name: _____

Time limit: 5 minutes

Draw the requested note, stem, and flag, as appropriate, in the following examples.

Example: Given: 𝅝 =

Answer: 𝅗𝅥 = ♫♫

How many eighth notes?

1.   𝅝 = How many quarter notes? _____

2.   𝅘𝅥. = How many sixteenth notes? _____

3.   ♪. = How many sixteenth notes? _____

4.   ▭ = How many quarter notes? _____

5.   𝅗𝅥 = How many sixteenth notes? _____

6.   𝅘𝅥. = How many eighth notes? _____

7.   𝅝. = How many quarter notes? _____

8.   ♪. = How many thirty-second notes? _____

9.   ▭ = How many eighth notes? _____

10.   𝅘𝅥 = How many sixteenth notes? _____

Answers on page 73

Name: _____   Time limit: 5 minutes

Translate each given note value into the requested grouping. Please use beams.

Example: Given: Answer:

                into eighth-note triplets

1.   𝅝   into quarter-note triplets   _____

2.   𝅗𝅥.   into eighth-note triplets   _____

3.   𝅝   into eighth-note quintuplets   _____

4.   𝅘𝅥   into quarter-note triplets   _____

5.   𝅝   into quarter-note sextuplets   _____

6.   𝅘𝅥   into eighth-note quintuplets   _____

7.   𝅘𝅥   into eighth-note triplets   _____

Answers on page 74

Provide foreground and background levels for each of the given meters. Label each example as simple or compound and duple, triple, or quadruple.

Example: Given: Answer:

$$\frac{2}{4}$$ $$\frac{2}{4}$$ ♩ ♩   foreground
                                                    background

simple, duple

1. $$\frac{9}{8}$$ _____   foreground
                                                         background

      _____

2. $$\frac{4}{2}$$ _____   foreground
                                                         background

      _____

3. $$\frac{3}{8}$$ _____   foreground
                                                         background

      _____

4. $$\frac{6}{4}$$ _____   foreground
                                                         background

      _____

5. $$\frac{3}{4}$$ _____   foreground
                                                         background

      _____

6. $\dfrac{12}{8}$ _____ foreground
                                                   background

    _____

7. $\dfrac{4}{8}$ _____ foreground
                                                   background

    _____

8. $\dfrac{2}{2}$ _____ foreground
                                                   background

    _____

9. $\dfrac{6}{8}$ _____ foreground
                                                   background

    _____

10. $\dfrac{2}{4}$ _____ foreground
                                                   background

    _____

Answers on pages 75-76

Name: _____   Time limit: 15 minutes

Identify the meter of the following examples by adding a meter sign and bar lines to each example.

Some examples begin with a downbeat, some begin with a pickup.

Some examples may work in more than one meter. You are responsible for choosing one possible meter.

1.

2.

3.

4.

5.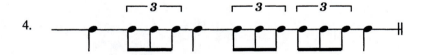

6.

7.

8.

9.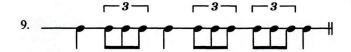

10.

11.

12.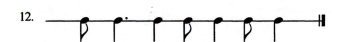

Answers on pages 77-78

Name: _____

Time limit: 10 minutes

Identify the meter of the following examples by adding a meter sign and bar lines to each example.

Some examples begin with a downbeat, some begin with a pickup.

Some examples may work in more than one meter. You are responsible for choosing
one possible meter.

1.

2.

3.

4.

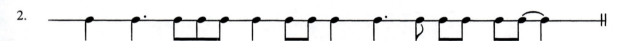

5.

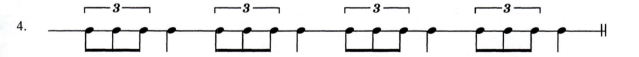

Answers on page 79

Name: _____

1. Write the requested pitches or rests in the given clefs. Be careful to put stems and flags on in the right direction.

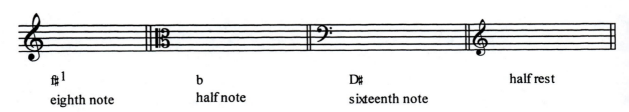

f♯¹   b   D♯   half rest

eighth note   half note   sixteenth note

2. Provide foreground and background levels for each of the given meters. Label each example as simple or compound and duple, triple, or quadruple.

Example: Given:

$\frac{2}{4}$

Answer:

foreground
background

simple, duple

$\frac{6}{8}$ _____

$\frac{4}{2}$ _____

3. Identify the meter of the following examples by adding a meter signature and bar lines. Examples
   may begin on a downbeat or with a pickup.

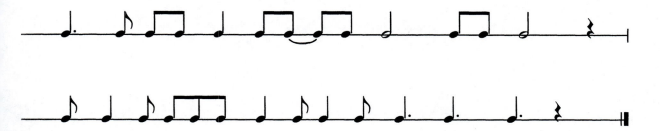

Answers on pages 80-81

In the space provided, draw two of the pitched and unpitched duration symbols given below.
Label each symbol with its correct name.

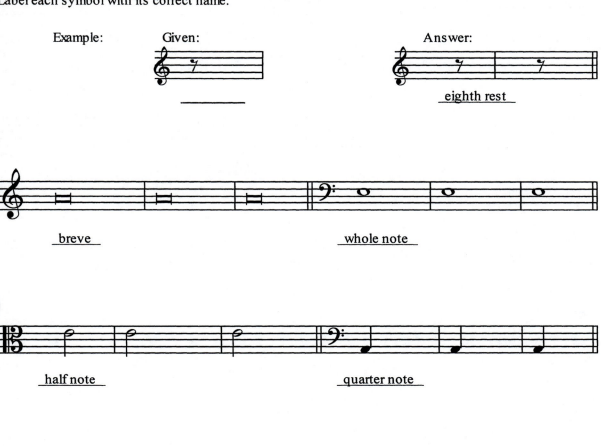

Example: Given: Answer:

eighth rest

breve   whole note

half note   quarter note

eighth note   sixteenth note

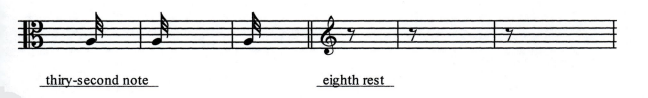

thiry-second note   eighth rest

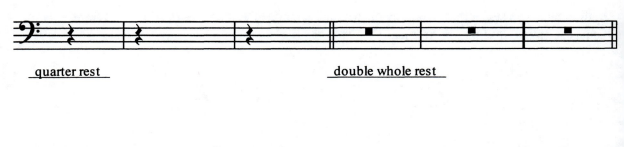

quarter rest   double whole rest

eighth rest   half rest

sixteenth rest   whole rest

Name the following symbols.

Example: Given: Answer:

_____   eighth rest

half rest   quarter note   thirty-second note   whole note   sixty-fourth note   breve

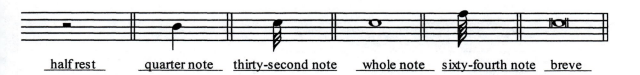

quarter rest   sixteenth note   thirty-second rest   half note   sixteenth rest   whole rest

eighth note   double whole rest   half rest   quarter note   eighth rest   sixteenth note

Write the requested symbols in the given clefs. Be careful to put stems and flags on in the right direction.

| a^1 | b | f^1 | half rest |
| quarter note | half note | eighth note | |

| sixteenth rest | breve rest | g^2 | whole rest |
| | | quarter note | |

| d | $f\#^2$ | $b\flat$ | quarter rest |
| quarter note | eighth note | sixteenth note | |

| c^1 | a | quarter rest | $f\#^2$ |
| sixteenth note | eighth note | | whole note |

| half rest | F | $a\flat^1$ | e^1 |
| | sixteenth note | eighth note | half note |

| D | b^2 | a^1 | b |
| whole note | half note | eighth note | half note |

Put stems on the following quarter notes. Choose stem direction **carefully** for the third-line notes, looking at the surrounding notes.

Draw the requested note, stem, and flag, as appropriate, in the following examples.

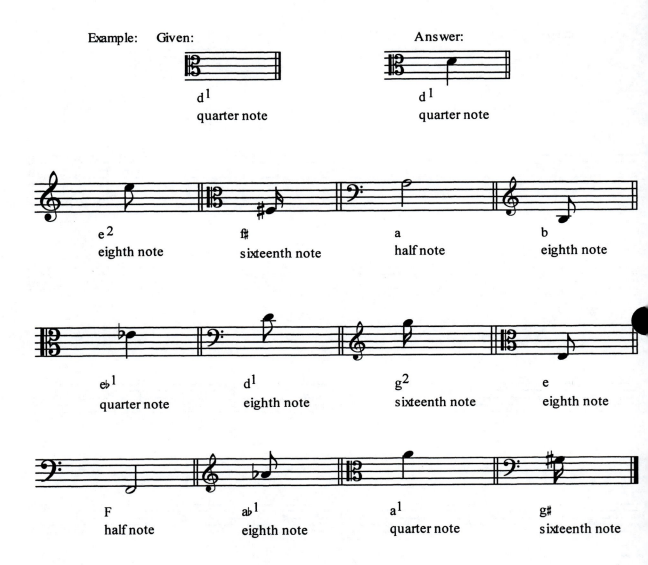

Draw the requested note, stem, and flag, as appropriate, in the following examples.

Example: Given:

♩ =

How many eighth notes?

Answer:

1.   o = How many quarter notes?

2.   ♩. = How many sixteenth notes?

3.   ♪. = How many sixteenth notes?

4.   𝅄 = How many quarter notes?

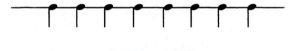

5.   𝅗𝅥 = How many sixteenth notes?

6.   ♩. = How many eighth notes?

7.   o. = How many quarter notes?

8.   ♪. = How many thirty-second notes?

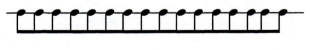

9.   𝅄 = How many eighth notes?

10.   ♩ = How many sixteenth notes?

Translate each given note value into the requested grouping. Please use beams.

Example: Given: Answer:

into eighth-note triplets

1.   into quarter-note triplets

2.   into eighth-note triplets

3.   into eighth-note quintuplets

4.   into quarter-note triplets

5.   into quarter-note sextuplets

6.   into eighth-note quintuplets

7.   into eighth-note triplets

Provide foreground and background levels for each of the given meters. Label each example as simple or compound and duple, triple, or quadruple.

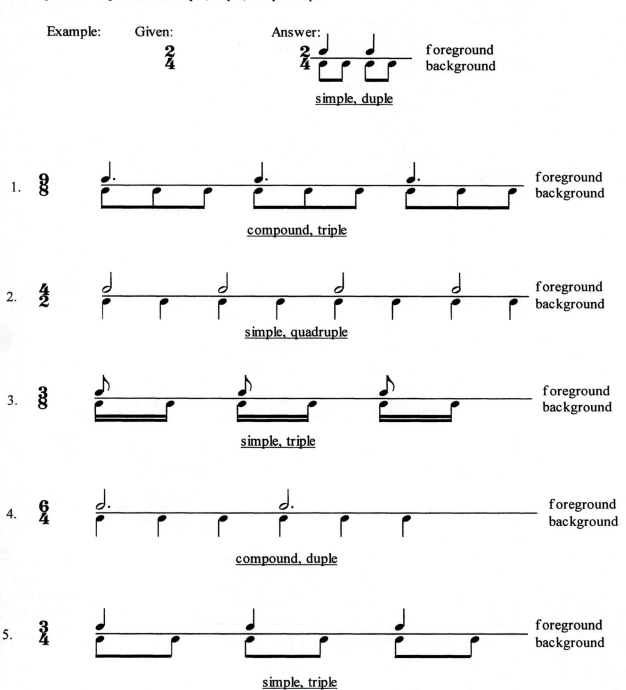

6.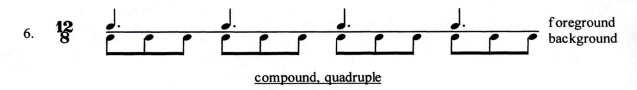

compound, quadruple

7.

simple, quadruple

8.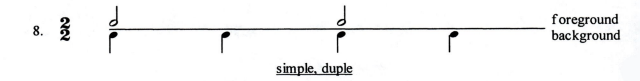

simple, duple

9.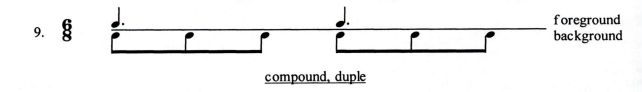

compound, duple

10.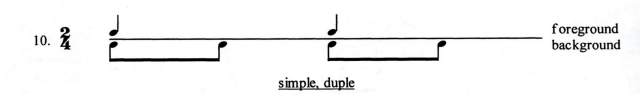

simple, duple

Identify the meter of the following examples by adding a meter sign and bar lines to each example.

Some examples begin with a downbeat, some begin with a pickup.

Some examples may work in more than one meter. You are responsible for choosing one possible meter.

1.   Also possible: $\frac{2}{4}$ $\frac{2}{2}$

2.   Also possible: $\frac{3}{8}$ $\frac{12}{8}$

3.

4.   Also possible: $\frac{2}{4}$

5.   Also possible: $\frac{3}{8}$ $\frac{12}{8}$

6.   Also possible: $\frac{4}{4}$ $\frac{2}{2}$

7.    Also possible: $\frac{3}{8}$ $\frac{12}{8}$

8.    Also possible: $\frac{3}{8}$ $\frac{12}{8}$

9. 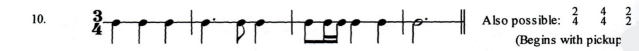   Also possible: $\frac{3}{4}$

10. 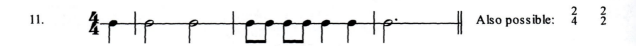   Also possible: $\frac{2}{4}$ $\frac{4}{4}$ $\frac{2}{2}$
(Begins with pickup

11.   Also possible: $\frac{2}{4}$ $\frac{2}{2}$

12.   Also possible: $\frac{6}{8}$ $\frac{12}{8}$

Identify the meter of the following examples by adding a meter sign and bar lines to each example.

Some examples begin with a downbeat, some begin with a pickup.

Some examples may work in more than one meter. You are responsible for choosing
one possible meter.

1.

2.

3.

4.

5.

1. Write the requested pitches or rests in the given clefs. Be careful to put stems and flags on in the right direction.

f♯ 1   b   D♯   half rest

eighth note   half note   sixteenth note

2. Provide foreground and background levels for each of the given meters. Label each example as simple or compound and duple, triple, or quadruple.

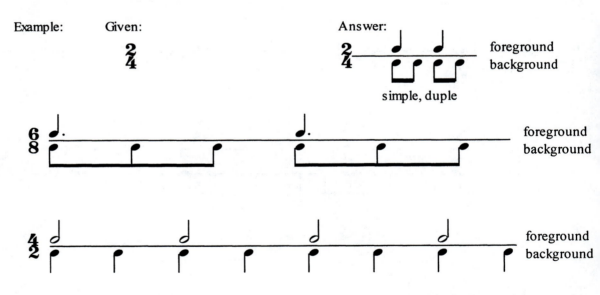

PRACTICE QUIZ ANSWERS
(continued)

3. Identify the meter of the following examples by adding a meter signature and bar lines. Examples may begin on a downbeat or with a pickup.

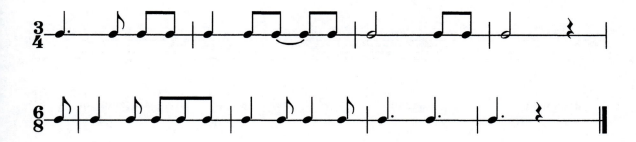

Name: _____

1. Write the requested pitches or rests in the given clefs. Be careful to put stems and flags on in the
   right direction. (2 points each)

c#   f¹   g²   F
quarter note   eighth note   half note   sixteenth note

2. Provide foreground and background levels for each of the given meters. Label each example as
   simple or compound and duple, triple, or quadruple. (3 points each)

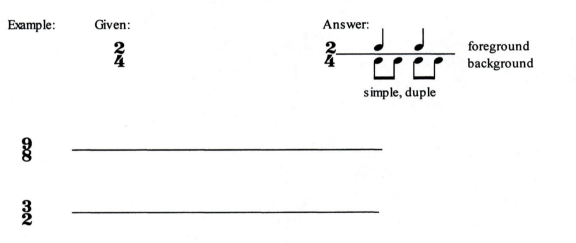

Example: Given: Answer: foreground
                $\frac{2}{4}$ $\frac{2}{4}$ background

                                                simple, duple

   $\frac{9}{8}$ _____

   $\frac{3}{2}$ _____

3. Identify the meter of the following examples by adding a meter signature and bar lines. Examples
   may begin on a downbeat or with a pickup. (3 points each)

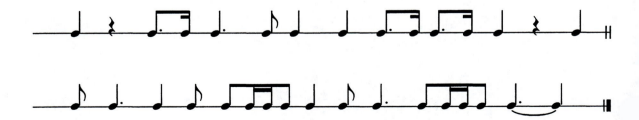

CHAPTER THREE   Major Scales

The term *scale* derives from the Italian word for ladder (*la scala*) and is an abstraction that explains the collection of pitches that occur in a musical composition to define a key.

1.   Scales: General Information

Most pieces of Western music from the common practice period (approximately 1700-1900 C.E.) use either major or minor scales as their basis. This means that the most frequently used pitches in a given piece, if gathered together and arranged by step and half step, would form a major or minor scale.

A scale is a series of steps and half steps bounded by an octave. Most scales are the same going up and coming down.

A scale comprised entirely of half steps is called a chromatic scale. Most of the time, notes that are sharped lead to the following note name (for example, G# leads to A; A# leads to B; B# leads to C#). Most of the time, notes that are flatted lead to the preceding note name (for example, A♭ leads to G; G♭ leads to F; F♭ leads to E♭).

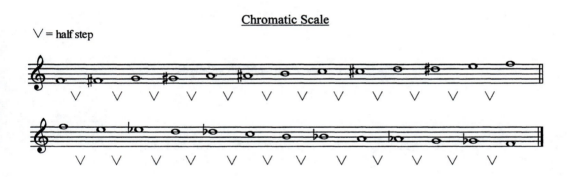

A scale comprised entirely of whole steps is called a whole-tone scale.

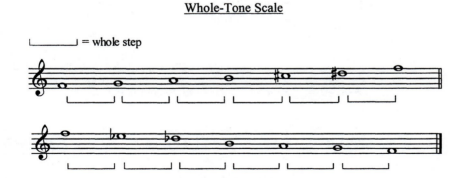

2.   Scale Degrees

The major scale uses seven adjacent pitches in a prescribed pattern of half steps and whole steps. The seven pitches that comprise all major scales are called *diatonic*, which means "belonging to the scale". The other five pitches are called *chromatic*, which means "outside of the scale". The seven pitches of the major scale have *numerical* and *proper* names. All major scales have one of each of the seven letter names: A, B, C, D, E, F, and G.

Scale Degree	Name	Derivation
$\hat{1}$	tonic	The primary *tone* of the scale.
$\hat{2}$	supertonic	The tone *above* the tonic.
$\hat{3}$	mediant	The tone *midway* between the tonic and the dominant.
$\hat{4}$	subdominant	The tone a perfect fifth *below* the tonic.
$\hat{5}$	dominant	The tone a perfect fifth above the tonic; the most *important* pitch after the tonic.
$\hat{6}$	submediant	The tone *midway* between the tonic and the subdominant.
$\hat{7}$	leading tone	The tone that *leads* to the tonic.
$\hat{8}$	tonic	The tone an octave above the primary tone.

Drill: Say the names of the notes of the major scale, in ascending and descending order: tonic, supertonic, mediant, subdominant, dominant, submediant, leading tone, tonic; tonic, leading tone, submediant, dominant, subdominant, mediant, supertonic, tonic. Be sure you can say them quickly without looking at the names. Be sure to say them while clapping a steady beat.

Drill: Say the scale degrees and names of the notes in the major scale, in ascending and descending order: $\hat{1}$ tonic, $\hat{2}$ supertonic, $\hat{3}$ mediant, $\hat{4}$ subdominant, $\hat{5}$ dominant, $\hat{6}$ submediant, $\hat{7}$ leading tone, $\hat{8}$ tonic; $\hat{8}$ tonic, $\hat{7}$ leading tone, $\hat{6}$ submediant, $\hat{5}$ dominant, $\hat{4}$ subdominant, $\hat{3}$ mediant, $\hat{2}$ supertonic, $\hat{1}$ tonic. Be sure you can say these quickly without looking at the numbers or names. Be sure to say them while clapping a steady beat.

Homework Assignment #1, p. 91

3.   Pattern

All major scales have seven diatonic pitches arranged in the following pattern of half steps (hs) and whole steps (ws):

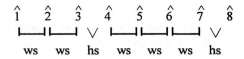

A portion of the piano keyboard is replicated below to remind you that there are no half steps between E and F or between B and C.

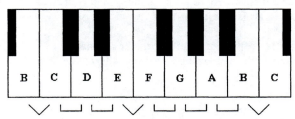

Major scales are defined by their pattern of steps and half steps. To build a major scale above any pitch, simply follow the prescribed pattern.

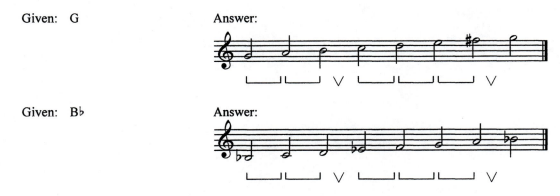

85

Drill: Practice building major scales beginning on C, C#, D♭, D, E♭, E, F, F#, G♭, G, A♭, A, B♭, B, and C♭. Clap a steady beat while saying the note names. Begin slowly and think carefully about half steps and whole steps.

Homework Assignments #2 and #3, pp. 92-94

4.   Key Signatures

Most pieces of Western music written in the common practice period (1700-1900 C.E.) rely primarily on the diatonic notes of a specific major scale. Therefore, a piece of music is said to be "in" E Major. This usually means that the majority of its pitches, especially at its beginning and ending, are found in the E Major scale.

As a convenience, musicians gather together the accidentals at the beginning of every staff of music for an entire composition. These collections are called *key signatures*.

The order of these collected accidentals is by perfect fifth (an interval of five letter names and seven half steps).

The key signature of E Major, a scale with four sharps, adds the sharps by ascending perfect fifths and arranges them by alternating descending perfect fourths and ascending perfect fifths.

E major

The fifth relationship between scales that share six pitches makes memorization easy. Remember that because of the half steps between E/F and B/C, fifths involving the pitches F and B need an accidental to be perfect fifths. (B up to F# is a perfect fifth; F down to B♭ is a perfect fifth.)

Flats are added by descending perfect fifth. For example, the key signature of D♭ Major, a scale with five flats, adds the flats by descending perfect fifths and arranges them by alternating ascending perfect fourths and descending perfect fifths.

D♭ major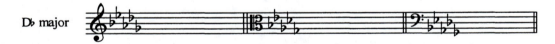

Homework Assignment #4, p. 95

86

There is a single correct way of writing key signatures. Look carefully at the following key signatures for the keys of C# major (seven sharps) and C♭ major (seven flats). This is the only proper way to write these key signatures.

Drill: Practice saying aloud the seven sharps and seven flats, in order, until you can recite them very quickly, clapping a steady beat each time. Be sure to say "F#", "C#", and so on, rather than "F", "C", and so on. Practice writing the seven sharps and seven flats in treble, alto, and bass clefs on the staff below.

5.   Circle of Fifths

The circle of fifths is a convenient way to show the relationships between major keys. Major keys whose tonics are related by perfect fifth have all but one note in common. For example, D major and A major are related by perfect fifth and contain six common pitches (D, E, F#, A, B, and C#). They differ in that D major contains the pitch G and A major contains the pitch G#.

Three pairs of keys are shown overlapping at the bottom of the circle. These pairs are enharmonic equivalents of each other: they sound the same but are notated differently.

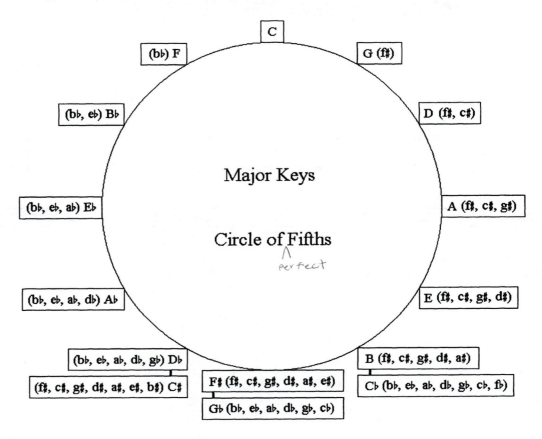

Drill: Practice saying aloud the fifteen major keys in perfect fifth order until you can do this very quickly, clapping a steady beat each time. Begin with C major and continue by ascending fifths, stopping at C# major. Begin again with C major and continue by descending fifths, stopping at C♭ major.

Drill: Practice saying aloud the fifteen major keys in perfect fifth order, with the number of accidentals in their key signatures. Practice until you can do this very quickly, clapping a steady beat each time. Begin with C major and continue by ascending fifths, stopping at C# major (e.g. C major, zero sharps or flats; G major, 1 sharp; D major, 2 sharps, and so on). Begin again with C major and continue by descending fifths, stopping at C♭ major (e.g. C major, zero sharps or flats; F major, 1 flat; B♭ major, 2 flats; and so on).

Homework Assignment #5, p. 96

Drill: Identify the keys of the following movements of Beethoven String Quartets by looking at their key signatures. To verify the key of each movement, examine the pitches in the first few measures. See Op.18, No. 2, first movement (page (25) 1) and second movement (page (31) 7); Op.18, No.5, first movement (page (83) 1) and third movement (page 8 (90)); and Op.135, third movement (page 12 (200)) and fourth movement (page (201) 13).

Homework Assignments #6, #7, and #8, pp. 97-99

In order to effectively analyze music, musicians must be fluent with key signatures and the names of the scale degrees.

Drill: Practice fluency by choosing one scale degree (tonic, supertonic, mediant, subdominant, dominant, submediant, or leading tone) and saying aloud each scale in the circle of fifths and that particular scale degree. For example, choosing $\hat{5}$, the dominant, work through the circle ascending and descending from C major as follows:

C major's dominant is G.
G major's dominant is D.
D major's dominant is A, and so on.

Stop at C# major and begin again through the descending circle:

C major's dominant is G.
F major's dominant is C.
Bb major's dominant is F, and so on.

Homework Assignments #9 and #10, pp. 100-101

PRACTICE QUIZ ON CHAPTER THREE, p. 102

Without referring to a written chart, fill in the blanks in the following sentences.

       Example: Question: The tonic is _____.

                         Answer: The tonic is $\hat{1}$.

1. The mediant is _____.

2. The leading tone is _____.

3. The supertonic is _____.

4. The submediant is _____.

5. The dominant is _____.

6. The subdominant is _____.

Without referring to a written chart, fill in the blanks in the following sentences.

       Example: Question: $\hat{1}$ is called the _____.

                         Answer: $\hat{1}$ is called the _tonic_.

1. $\hat{5}$ is called the _____.

2. $\hat{6}$ is called the _____.

3. $\hat{7}$ is called the _____.

4. $\hat{2}$ is called the _____.

5. $\hat{3}$ is called the _____.

6. $\hat{4}$ is called the _____.

7. $\hat{6}$ is called the _____.

Answers on page 103

Name: _____

Using half notes, write the following major scales in the requested clefs. *Do not use key signatures.*

Example: F major, treble clef

Answer:

FM

1. B♭ major, bass clef

2. E major, treble clef

3. B♭ major, bass clef

4. C♭ major, treble clef

5. G major, alto clef

6. D major, bass clef

7. G♭ major, treble clef

8. D♭ major, bass clef

9. F♯ major, treble clef

10. B major, alto clef

11. A♭ major, bass clef

12. A major, treble clef

13. C♯ major, bass clef

Answers on pages 104-105

Name: _____

For every pitch listed below, name the perfect fifth above and below.

Given: C#   _____

Answer: C#   <u>G# and F#</u>

1. D _____

2. F# _____

3. E♭ _____

4. B _____

5. D# _____

6. C♭ _____

7. F _____

8. A♭ _____

For every major key listed below, name the major keys a perfect fifth above and a perfect fifth below.

Given: C major   _____

Answer: C major   <u>G major and F major</u>

1. E♭ major _____

2. D major _____

3. B major _____

4. D♭ major _____

5. C♭ major _____

6. F# major _____

7. B♭ major _____

8. G major _____

9. A♭ major _____

10. E major _____

Answers on page 106

Name: _____

For every major key listed below, write the accidentals in order in the given clef.

Example:
Given: F major   Answer: F major

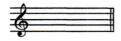

1. B♭ major

2. D major

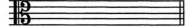

3. B major

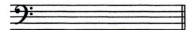

4. D♭ major

5. C♭ major

6. F# major

7. B♭ major

8. G major

9. A♭ major

10. E major

11. G♭ major

12. A major

13. C# major

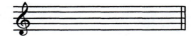

Answers on page 107

Name: _____

Time limit: 10 minutes

Without looking at the circle in the text, write in all of the major keys with their associated accidentals.

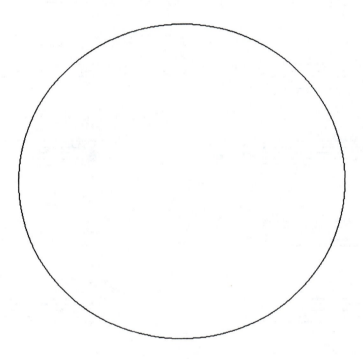

Answers on page 108

Name:_____

Time limit: 15 minutes

For every major key listed below, write the key signature in order in the given clef.

Example:
Given: F♯ major, bass clef

Answer: F♯ major, bass clef

1. B major, bass clef

2. D♭ major, alto clef

3. C♯ major, treble clef

4. F major, bass clef

5. E major, treble clef

6. G♭ major, bass clef

7. B♭ major, treble clef

8. G major, bass clef

9. C♭ major, alto clef

10. A major, treble clef

11. B♭ major, bass clef

12. A♭ major, treble clef

13. D major, bass clef

Answers on page 109

Name: _____

Time limit: 10 minutes

Fill in the blanks with the proper number and accidentals.

Example: Question: E major has a key signature of _____.

Answer: E major has a key signature of <u>4 sharps – F# C# G# D#</u>.

1. F# major has a key signature of _____.

2. B♭ major has a key signature of _____.

3. D major has a key signature of _____.

4. D♭ major has a key signature of _____.

5. G major has a key signature of _____.

6. A♭ major has a key signature of _____.

7. C major has a key signature of _____.

8. B major has a key signature of _____.

9. G♭ major has a key signature of _____.

10. A major has a key signature of _____.

11. F major has a key signature of _____.

12. C# major has a key signature of _____.

13. E♭ major has a key signature of _____.

Answers on page 110

Name: _____   Time limit: 10 minutes

Give the name of the major scale described in each statement.

        Example: Question: The major key with four sharps is _____.

                            Answer: The major key with four sharps is __E major__.

1.   The major key with six sharps is _____.

2.   The major key with three flats is _____.

3.   The major key with two sharps is _____.

4.   The major key with five flats is _____.

5.   The major key with one sharp is _____.

6.   The major key with seven flats is _____.

7.   The major key with three sharps is _____.

8.   The major key with two flats is _____.

9.   The major key with four sharps is _____.

10. The major key with one flat is _____.

11. The major key with five sharps is _____.

12. The major key with six flats is _____.

13. The major key with four flats is _____.

Answers on page 111

Name: _____

Fill in the blanks in the sentences below.

    Example: Question: The supertonic of E major is _____.

                Answer: The supertonic of E major is _____F#_____.

1. The mediant of D♭ major is _____.

2. The leading tone of A major is _____.

3. The supertonic of B major is _____.

4. The submediant of A major is _____.

5. The supertonic of A♭ major is _____.

6. The dominant of B major is _____.

7. The tonic of F major is _____.

8. The subdominant of D major is _____.

9. The mediant of E♭ major is _____.

10. The leading tone of C# major is _____.

11. The dominant of G major is _____.

12. The submediant of C♭ major is _____.

13. The subdominant of E major is _____.

14. The mediant of C major is _____.

15. The leading tone of G♭ major is _____.

Answers on page 112

Fill in the blanks in the sentences below.

       Example: Question: The supertonic of E major is _____.

                       Answer: The supertonic of E major is _____F#_____.

1. The mediant of A major is _____.

2. The leading tone of E♭ major is _____.

3. The supertonic of G♭ major is _____.

4. The submediant of B major is _____.

5. The supertonic of D major is _____.

6. The dominant of A♭ major is _____.

7. The tonic of F# major is _____.

8. The subdominant of E major is _____.

9. The mediant of B♭ major is _____.

10. The leading tone of G major is _____.

11. The dominant of D♭ major is _____.

12. The submediant of C# major is _____.

13. The subdominant of F major is _____.

14. The mediant of C♭ major is _____.

15. The leading tone of C major is _____.

Answers on page 113

Name: _____

1. For every major key listed below, write the key signature in the given clef.

Example:
Given:

Answer:

Bb:

Bb:

Bb: A: Cb: B:

1.   Fill in the blanks in the sentences below.

     a.   The mediant of B major is _____.

     b.   The leading tone of Ab major is _____.

     c.   The supertonic of E major is _____.

     d.   The submediant of Db major is _____.

     e.   The supertonic of F# major is _____.

     f.   The dominant of Bb major is _____.

     g.   The subdominant of C# major is _____.

Answers on page 114

Without referring to a written chart, fill in the blanks in the following sentences.

       Example: Question: The tonic is _____.

                       Answer: The tonic is __$\hat{1}$__.

1. The mediant is ___$\hat{3}$___.

2. The leading tone is ___$\hat{7}$___.

3. The supertonic is ___$\hat{2}$___.

4. The submediant is ___$\hat{6}$___.

5. The dominant is ___$\hat{5}$___.

6. The subdominant is ___$\hat{4}$___.

Without referring to a written chart, fill in the blanks in the following sentences.

       Example: Question: $\hat{1}$ is called the _____.

                       Answer: $\hat{1}$ is called the _tonic_.

1. $\hat{5}$ is called the _dominant_.

2. $\hat{6}$ is called the _submediant_.

3. $\hat{7}$ is called the _leading tone_.

4. $\hat{2}$ is called the _supertonic_.

5. $\hat{3}$ is called the _mediant_.

6. $\hat{4}$ is called the _subdominant_.

7. $\hat{6}$ is called the _submediant_.

Using half notes, write the following major scales in the requested clefs. *Do not use key signatures.*

Example: F major, treble clef

Answer:

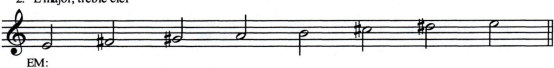

FM:

1. B♭ major, bass clef

B♭M:

2. E major, treble clef

EM:

3. B♭ major, bass clef

B♭M:

4. C♭ major, treble clef

C♭M:

5. G major, alto clef

GM:

HOMEWORK ANSWERS #2
(continued)

6. D major, bass clef

DM:

7. G♭ major, treble clef

G♭M:

8. D♭ major, bass clef

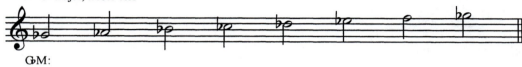

D♭M:

9. F♯ major, treble clef

F♯M:

10. B major, alto clef

BM

11. A♭ major, bass clef

A♭M:

12. A major, treble clef

AM:

13. C♯ major, bass clef

C♯M:

For every pitch listed below, name the perfect fifth above and below.

Given: C#   _____

Answer: C#   ___G# and F#___

1. D _____A and G_____   5. D# _____A# and G#_____

8. F# _____C# and B_____   6. Cb _____Gb and Fb_____

9. Eb _____Bb and Ab_____   7. F   _____C and Bb_____

10. B _____F# and E_____   8. Ab _____Eb and Db_____

For every major key listed below, name the major keys a perfect fifth above and a perfect fifth below.

Given: C major   _____

Answer: C major   ___G major and F major___

1.   Eb major   __Bb major and Ab major__

2.   D major   __A major and G major__

3.   B major   __F# major and E major__

4.   Db major   __Ab major and Gb major__

5.   Cb major   __Gb major and Fb major__

6.   F# major   __C# major and B major__

7.   Bb major   __F major and Eb major__

8.   G major   __D major and C major__

9.   Ab major   __Eb major and Db major__

10. E major   __B major and A major__

For every major key listed below, write the accidentals in order in the given clef.

Example:
Given: F major

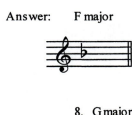

Answer: F major

1. B♭ major

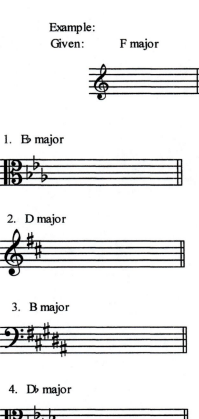

2. D major

3. B major

4. D♭ major

5. C♭ major

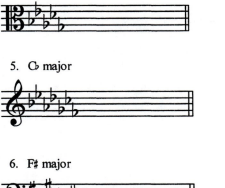

6. F♯ major

7. B♭ major

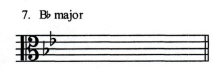

8. G major

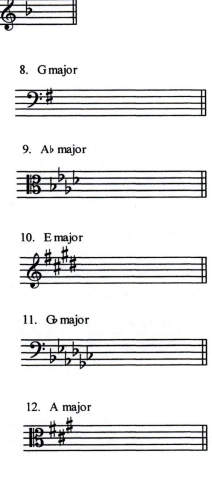

9. A♭ major

10. E major

11. G♭ major

12. A major

13. C♯ major

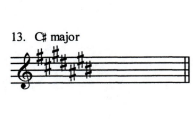

Without looking at the circle in the text, write in all of the major keys with their associated accidentals.

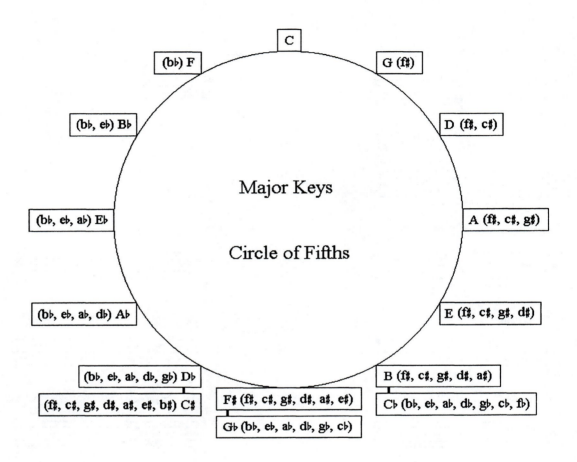

For every major key listed below, write the key signature in the given clef.

Example:
Given: F♯ major, bass clef
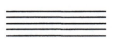

Answer: F♯ major, bass clef

1. B major, bass clef
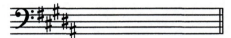

8. G major, bass clef

2. D♭ major, alto clef
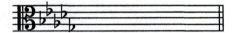

9. C♭ major, alto clef
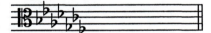

3. C♯ major, treble clef
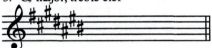

10. A major, treble clef
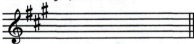

4. F major, bass clef
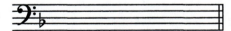

11. E♭ major, bass clef

5. E major, treble clef
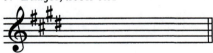

12. A♭ major, treble clef
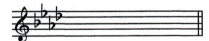

6. G♭ major, bass clef

13. D major, bass clef
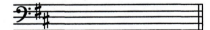

7. B♭ major, treble clef

Fill in the blanks with the proper number and accidentals.

       Example: Question: E major has a key signature of _____.

                      Answer: E major has a key signature of <u>4 sharps – F# C# G# D#</u>.

1. F# major has a key signature of <u>6 sharps – F# C# G# D# A# E#</u>.

2. B♭ major has a key signature of <u>2 flats – B♭ E♭</u>.

3. D major has a key signature of <u>2 sharps – F# C#</u>.

4. D♭ major has a key signature of <u>5 flats – B♭ E♭ A♭ D♭ G♭</u>.

5. G major has a key signature of <u>1 sharp – F#</u>.

6. A♭ major has a key signature of <u>4 flats – B♭ E♭ A♭ D♭</u>.

7. C major has a key signature of <u>0 flats and 0 sharps</u>.

8. B major has a key signature of <u>5 sharps – F# C# G# D# A#</u>.

9. G♭ major has a key signature of <u>6 flats – B♭ E♭ A♭ D♭ G♭ C♭</u>.

10. A major has a key signature of <u>3 sharps – F# C# G#</u>.

11. F major has a key signature of <u>1 flat - B♭</u>.

12. C# major has a key signature of <u>7 sharps – F# C# G# D# A# E# B#</u>.

13. E♭ major has a key signature of <u>3 flats – B♭ E♭ A♭</u>.

Give the name of the major scale described in each statement.

Example: Question: The major key with four sharps is _____.

                  Answer: The major key with four sharps is ___E major___.

1. The major key with six sharps is ___F# major___.

2. The major key with three flats is ___E♭ major___.

3. The major key with two sharps is ___D major___.

4. The major key with five flats is ___D♭ major___.

5. The major key with one sharp is ___G major___.

6. The major key with seven flats is ___C♭ major___.

7. The major key with three sharps is ___A major___.

8. The major key with two flats is ___B♭ major___.

9. The major key with four sharps is ___E major___.

10. The major key with one flat is ___F major___.

11. The major key with five sharps is ___B major___.

12. The major key with six flats is ___G♭ major___.

13. The major key with four flats is ___A♭ major___.

Fill in the blanks in the sentences below.

Example: Question: The supertonic of E major is _____.

            Answer: The supertonic of E major is _____F#_____.

1. The mediant of D♭ major is _____F_____.

2. The leading tone of A major is _____G#_____.

3. The supertonic of B major is _____C#_____.

4. The submediant of A major is _____F#_____.

5. The supertonic of A♭ major is _____B♭_____.

6. The dominant of B major is _____F#_____.

7. The tonic of F major is _____F_____.

8. The subdominant of D major is ____G_____.

9. The mediant of E♭ major is _____G_____.

10. The leading tone of C# major is ___B#_____.

11. The dominant of G major is _____D_____.

12. The submediant of C♭ major is ____A♭_____.

13. The subdominant of E major is ___A_____.

14. The mediant of C major is _____E_____.

15. The leading tone of G♭ major is ___F_____.

Fill in the blanks in the sentences below.

Example: Question: The supertonic of E major is _____.

                  Answer: The supertonic of E major is _____F#_____.

1. The mediant of A major is _____C#_____.

2. The leading tone of E♭ major is ____D_____.

3. The supertonic of G♭ major is ____A♭_____.

4. The submediant of B major is ____G#_____.

5. The supertonic of D major is ____E_____.

6. The dominant of A♭ major is _____E♭_____.

7. The tonic of F# major is _____F#_____.

8. The subdominant of E major is ___A_____.

9. The mediant of B♭ major is _____D_____.

10. The leading tone of G major is ___F#_____.

11. The dominant of D♭ major is _____A♭_____.

12. The submediant of C# major is ___A#_____.

13. The subdominant of F major is ___B♭_____.

14. The mediant of C♭ major is _____E♭_____.

15. The leading tone of C major is ___B_____.

1. For every major key listed below, write the key signature in the given clef.

Example:
Given: Answer:

B♭:   B♭:

B♭:   A: C♭:   B:

2. Fill in the blanks in the sentences below.

   a.   The mediant of B major is _____ D# _____.

   b.   The leading tone of A♭ major is ____ G _____.

   c.   The supertonic of E major is _____ F# _____.

   d.   The submediant of D♭ major is ____ B♭ _____.

   e.   The supertonic of F# major is ____ G# _____.

   f.   The dominant of B♭ major is _____ F _____.

   g.   The subdominant of C# major is ___ F# _____.

NAME: _____

1. For every major key listed below, write the key signature in the given clef. (2 points each)

   B major   G♭ major   D major   B♭ major

2. Fill in the blanks in the sentences below. (2 points each)

   a.   The supertonic of A major is _____.

   b.   The subdominant of D♭ major is _____.

   c.   The leading tone of E major is _____.

   d.   The mediant of C♭ major is _____.

   e.   The dominant of F# major is _____.

   f.   The submediant of E♭ major is _____.

   g.   The subdominant of A♭ major is _____.

CHAPTER FOUR   Intervals

Musicians hear and see relationships between pitches. Intervals are the distances between pitches.

1.   Intervals: General Information

An interval is a description of the relationship between two notes. Two notes that sound simultaneously are called a harmonic or vertical interval. Two notes that sound successively are called a melodic or horizontal interval.

A simple interval is a pair of notes whose relationship to each other encompasses an octave or less. A compound interval is a pair of notes whose relationship to each other encompasses more than an octave.

All intervals are given two labels: one describing number (based on alphabet names) and one describing type (based on quality).

2.   Simple Intervals: Number and Type

You should always identify an interval by determining its **number** first and its **type** second.

<u>Simple Intervals</u>

Number	Name
1	prime (unison)
2	second
3	third
4	fourth
5	fifth
6	sixth
7	seventh
8	octave (8va)

The letter names A, B, C, D, E, F, and G determine the number of an interval. Count the number of letter names to determine the number of an interval:

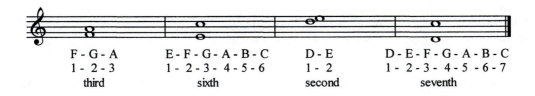

F - G - A	E - F - G - A - B - C	D - E	D - E - F - G - A - B - C
1 - 2 - 3	1 - 2 - 3 - 4 - 5 - 6	1 - 2	1 - 2 - 3 - 4 - 5 - 6 - 7
third	sixth	second	seventh

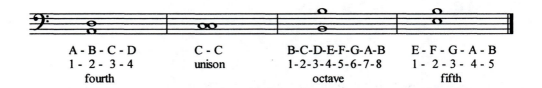

A - B - C - D	C - C	B-C-D-E-F-G-A-B	E - F - G - A - B
1 - 2 - 3 - 4	unison	1-2-3-4-5-6-7-8	1 - 2 - 3 - 4 - 5
fourth		octave	fifth

<u>Drill:</u>   Beginning on the note A and clapping in a steady rhythm, say all of the simple interval numbers and letter names above and then below A:

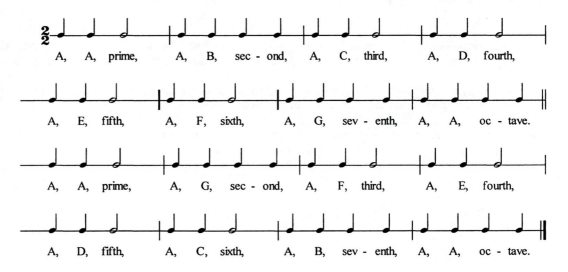

Continue this drill beginning on B, C, D, E, F, and G.

Homework Assignment #1, p. 129

The five most common interval types are:

Interval Types	Symbol
perfect interval	P
major interval	M
minor interval	m or $\overline{m}$ *
augmented interval	A
diminished interval	d

* The difference between uppercase and lowercase is very clear in printing (M and m). To avoid confusion when writing by hand, use a line to indicate minor ($\overline{m}$).

Intervals may be doubly augmented or doubly diminished, but these intervals do not occur often in music.

The following simple intervals can be perfect, augmented, or diminished but *never* major or minor: unison (1), fourth (4), fifth (5), and octave (8).

Possible	Impossible
P1, A1	M1, m1, d1*
P4, A4, d4	M4, m4
P5, A5, d5	M5, m4
P8, A1	M8, m8

*There is no such interval as a "diminished unison." The two notes that make up a perfect unison cannot be brought closer to each other.

The following simple intervals can be major, minor, augmented, or diminished but *never* perfect: second (2), third (3), sixth (6), and seventh (7).

Possible	Impossible
d2, m2, M2, A2	P2
d3, m3, M3, A3	P3
d6, m6, M6, A6	P6
d7, m7, M7, A7	P7

3.   Simple Intervals: Identification

Interval type can be determined in two ways: (1) by counting half steps; and (2) by understanding the relationships of pitches in a major scale.

Interval Number and Type		Content
perfect prime	P1	no half steps
minor second	m2	1 half step
major second	M2	2 half steps (1 step)
minor third	m3	3 half steps (1 ½ steps)
major third	M3	4 half steps (2 steps)
perfect fourth	P4	5 half steps (2 ½ steps)
tritone*	tt	6 half steps (3 steps)
perfect fifth	P5	7 half steps (3 ½ steps)
minor sixth	m6	8 half steps (4 steps)
major sixth	M6	9 half steps (4 ½ steps)
minor seventh	m7	10 half steps (5 steps)
major seventh	M7	11 half steps (5 ½ steps)
perfect octave	P8	12 half steps (6 steps)

*A tritone is equivalent to an augmented fourth or a diminished fifth. It spans three (tri-) whole steps (tones).

119

Any **perfect** interval made a half step larger becomes **augmented**.

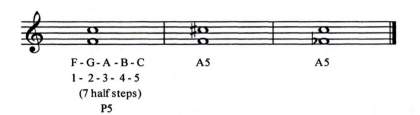

F - G - A - B - C
1 - 2 - 3 - 4 - 5
(7 half steps)
P5

In the key of F major, F (tonic) to C (dominant) is a P5; F to C# is a half step larger, thus an A5; F♭ to C is also a half step larger, thus an A5.

Any **perfect** interval made a half step smaller becomes **diminished**.

P5
(7 half steps)

In the key of F major, F (tonic) to C (dominant) is a P5; F# to C is a half step smaller, thus a d5; F to C♭ is also a half step smaller, thus a d5.

Any **major** interval made a half step larger becomes **augmented**.

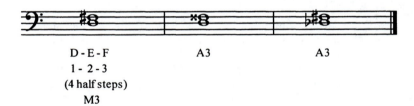

D - E - F
1 - 2 - 3
(4 half steps)
M3

In the key of D major, D (tonic) to F# (mediant) is a M3; D to F is a half step larger, thus an A3; D♭ to F# is also a half step larger, thus an A3.

Any **major** interval made a half step smaller becomes **minor**.

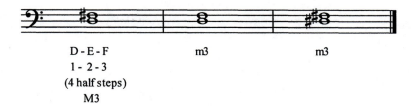

D - E - F   m3   m3
1 - 2 - 3
(4 half steps)
M3

In the key of D major, D (tonic) to F# (mediant) is a M3; therefore
D to F (a half step smaller) is a m3; D# to F# is also a half step smaller
than D to F# and is also a m3.

Any **major** interval made a whole step smaller becomes **diminished**.

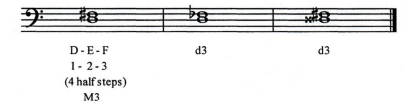

D - E - F   d3   d3
1 - 2 - 3
(4 half steps)
M3

In the key of D major, D (tonic) to F# (mediant) is a M3; D to F♭ is a
whole step smaller and thus a d3; D to F# is also a whole step smaller
and is also a d3.

Any **minor** interval made a half step larger becomes **major**.

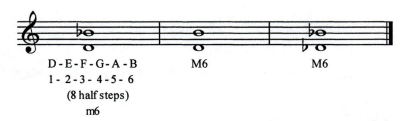

D - E - F - G - A - B   M6   M6
1 - 2 - 3 - 4 - 5 - 6
(8 half steps)
m6

In the key of D major, D (tonic) to B (submediant) is a M6; therefore,
D to B♭, a half step smaller, is a m6; D♭ to B♭, where the number of
half steps remains the same as in D to B, is also a M6.

Any **minor** interval made a half step smaller becomes **diminished**.

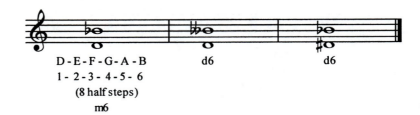

D - E - F - G - A - B   d6   d6
1 - 2 - 3 - 4 - 5 - 6
(8 half steps)
m6

In the key of D major, D (tonic) to B (submediant) is a M6, therefore,
D to B♭, a half step smaller, is a m6; D to B♭♭, a half step smaller again,
is thus a d6; D# to B♭, also a half step smaller than D to B♭, is also a d6.

Another way of determining interval type is through an understanding of the pitches that occur in the major scale. In any *ascending* major scale, the intervals between the tonic and the other members of the scale are always major or perfect.

<u>Intervals between the Tonic and Other Notes in the Ascending Major Scale</u>

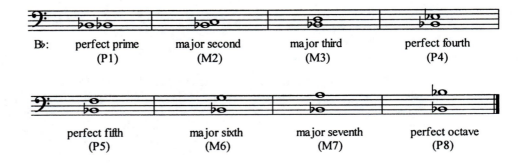

B♭:   perfect prime   major second   major third   perfect fourth
           (P1)   (M2)   (M3)   (P4)

    perfect fifth   major sixth   major seventh   perfect octave
           (P5)   (M6)   (M7)   (P8)

In any *descending* major scale, the intervals between the tonic and the other members of the scale are always minor or perfect.

<u>Intervals between the Tonic and Other Notes in the Descending Major Scale</u>

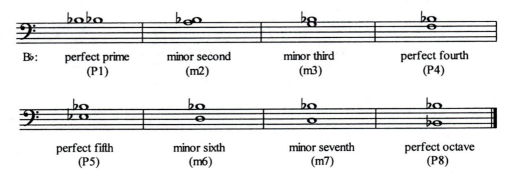

B♭:   perfect prime   minor second   minor third   perfect fourth
           (P1)   (m2)   (m3)   (P4)

    perfect fifth   minor sixth   minor seventh   perfect octave
           (P5)   (m6)   (m7)   (P8)

Drill: Sing the following exercise until you can perform it quickly without looking at it.

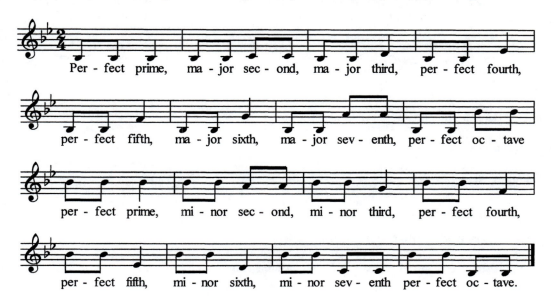

Drill: Sing the exercise given above, adding letter names to the interval types (see below). Sing this exercise in different keys.

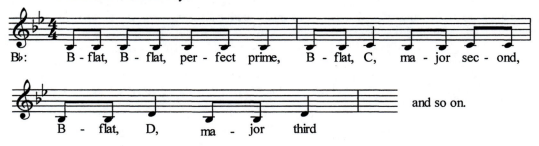

and so on.

Homework Assignment #2, p. 130

Intervals that do not occur in the major scale can be identified by relating them to intervals that occur in the major scale.

major intervals	+	1 half step	=	augmented intervals
(M2, M3, M6, M7)				(A2, A3, A6, A7)
minor intervals	+	1 half step	=	major intervals
(m2, m3, m6, m7)				(M2, M3, M6, M7)
perfect intervals	+	1 half step	=	augmented intervals
(P1, P4, P5, P8)				(A1, A4, A5, A8)
perfect intervals	-	1 half step	=	diminished intervals
(P4, P5, P8)				(d4, d5, d8)

minor intervals (m2, m3, m6, m7)	-	1 half step	=	diminished intervals (d2, d3, d6, d7)
major intervals (M2, M3, M6, M7)	-	1 half step	=	minor intervals (m2, m3, m6, m7)

The following is a simplification of the chart above:

<u>For seconds, thirds, sixths, and sevenths</u>

diminished ←±→ minor ←±→ Major ←±→ Augmented

<u>For unisons, fourths, fifths, and octaves</u>

diminished ←±→ Perfect ←±→ Augmented

<u>Summary</u>

All intervals can be made larger or smaller by increasing or decreasing the number of half steps they contain (with the exception of the perfect unison, which cannot be made smaller). All intervals can be correctly labeled by comparing them to known major scales.

Be very careful when you are working to identify the interval number first. The following pairs of intervals are examples where the number of half steps is the same, but the correct number of each interval is different.

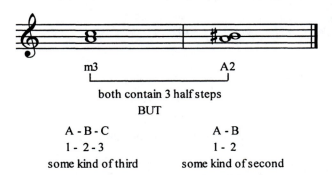

In the key of A major, A (tonic) to C# (mediant) is a M3;
therefore, A to C, a half step smaller, is a m3.
In the key of A major, A (tonic) to B (supertonic) is a M2;
therefore, A to B#, a half step larger, is an A2.

<u>Drill:</u> Identify by reading aloud the note names and proper interval labels for the intervals between all adjacent pairs of voices (Violin I and Violin II, Violin II and viola; viola and violoncello) in Beethoven's String Quartet Op. 59, No. 3, third movement, 14 (192), bottom line of page.

Homework Assignments #3 and #4, pp. 131-132

4. Building Simple Intervals

Always find the correct **letter name** to get the correct interval number before tackling the **type** when building intervals.

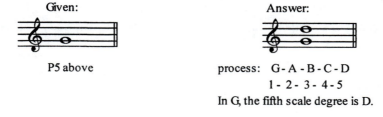

Given:

P5 above

Answer:

process: G- A - B - C - D
          1 - 2 - 3 - 4 - 5
In G, the fifth scale degree is D.

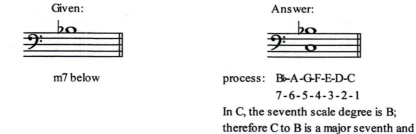

Given:

m7 below

Answer:

process: B♭-A-G-F-E-D-C
          7 - 6- 5- 4- 3- 2- 1
In C, the seventh scale degree is B;
therefore C to B is a major seventh and
C to B♭ is a minor seventh.

Once you have the correct note (letter name), relate the top or bottom note to a major scale you know.

Given:

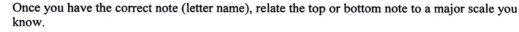

| M3 above | M2 below | d5 above | M7 below | d5 above |

Answers:

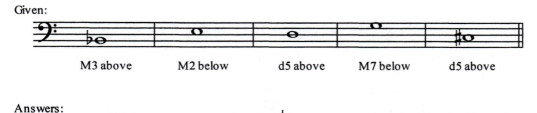

Homework Assignments #5, #6, and #7, pp. 133-135

5. Identifying Compound Intervals

A simple interval is a pair of notes that are one octave or less apart. A compound interval is a pair of notes that are more than one octave apart. In other words, a compound interval is a simple interval *plus* an octave or two octaves or three octaves, and so on.

To determine the number of a compound interval, remove the octave(s) to identify its simple equivalent, then add 7.

You should *always* identify a compound interval by determining its **simple number** first, its **type** second, and its **compound number** third.

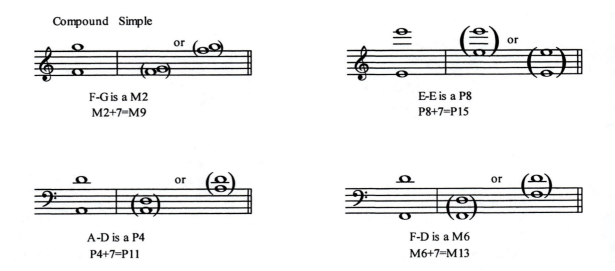

Compound   Simple

F-G is a M2
M2+7=M9

E-E is a P8
P8+7=P15

A-D is a P4
P4+7=P11

F-D is a M6
M6+7=M13

Table of Relationships between Simple and Compound Intervals

Compound Interval	Related Simple Interval	Simple +7 = Compound
8 octave (8ve)	1 prime	1 + 7 = 8
9 ninth	2 second	2 + 7 = 9
10 tenth	3 third	3 + 7 = 10
11 eleventh	4 fourth	4 + 7 = 11
12 twelfth	5 fifth	5 + 7 = 12
13 thirteenth	6 sixth	6 + 7 = 13
14 fourteenth	7 seventh	7 + 7 = 14
15 fifteenth (double 8ve)	8 octave (8ve)	8 + 7 = 15

Drill: Say aloud all simple intervals and their compound equivalents (1 becomes 8; 2 becomes 9; 3 becomes 10; and so on). Say aloud all compound intervals, from 9 to 15 and their simple equivalents (9 becomes 2; 10 becomes 3, and so on).

Homework Assignment #8, p. 136

6. Inversion of Simple Intervals

To invert intervals, simply change the relative position of the two notes, putting the note that was on top on the bottom, or vice versa.

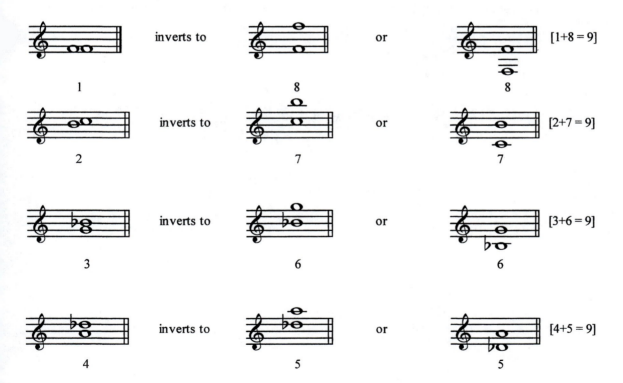

The magic number for inverting simple intervals is **nine.** Nine is the sum of the two interval numbers.

INVERSION OF SIMPLE INTERVALS

1	inverts to	8	1 + 8 = 9
2	inverts to	7	2 + 7 = 9
3	inverts to	6	3 + 6 = 9
4	inverts to	5	4 + 5 = 9
5	inverts to	4	5 + 4 = 9
6	inverts to	3	6 + 3 = 9
7	inverts to	2	7 + 2 = 9
8	inverts to	1	8 + 1 = 9

Drill: Say aloud the inversions of all simple intervals (1 inverts to 8; 2 inverts to 7; 3 inverts to 6; etc. and 8 inverts to 1; 7 inverts to 2; etc.)

Interval **types** invert simply and precisely.

Interval Type	Inversion
P perfect	P perfect
M major	m minor
m minor	M major
d diminished	A augmented
A augmented	d diminished

Drill: Say aloud the interval types and their inversions: perfect inverts to perfect; major inverts to minor; minor inverts to major; augmented inverts to diminished; diminished inverts to augmented.

The only exception to these rules concerns the augmented octave (A8).

There is no such interval as a diminished unison. Two notes that are exactly the same cannot be brought closer together.

Homework Assignment #9, p. 137

PRACTICE QUIZ ON CHAPTER FOUR, p. 138

Name: _____

Identify the following intervals by **number**.

Example: Given:  Answer: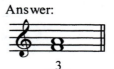

_3_

1. 2   2. 6   3. 5   4. 3   5. 7

6. 4   7. 8   8. 4   9. 2   10. 2

11. 6   12. 3   13. 1   14. 6   15. 4

16. 6   17. 4   18. 8   19. 3   20. 6

Answers on page 139

Name: _____

Time limit: 8 minutes

Identify the following intervals by **number** and **type**. All intervals will be either major or perfect.

1. ____   2. ____   3. ____   4. ____   5. ____

6. ____   7. ____   8. ____   9. ____   10. ____

11. ____   12. ____   13. ____   14. ____   15. ____

Answers on page 140

Name: _____   Time limit: 10 minutes

Identify the following intervals by **number** and **type**. Be sure to determine the **number** first.

Example: Given: Answer:

   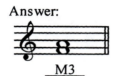

_____   _M3_

1. _____   2. _____   3. _____   4. _____   5. _____

6. _____   7. _____   8. _____   9. _____   10. _____

11. _____   12. _____   13. _____   14. _____   15. _____

16. _____   17. _____   18. _____   19. _____   20. _____

Answers on page 141

Name: _____   Time limit: 10 minutes

Identify the following intervals by **number** and **type**. Be sure to determine the **number** first.

Example: Given: Answer:

_____   P5

1. dim.3   2. _____   3. _____   4. _____   5. _____

6. _____   7. _____   8. _____   9. _____   10. _____

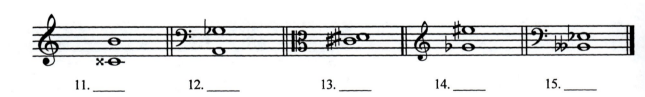

11. _____   12. _____   13. _____   14. _____   15. _____

Answers on page 142

Name: _____

Time limit: 10 minutes

Build the requested interval **above** the given note.

Example: Given:    Answer: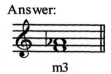

m3   m3

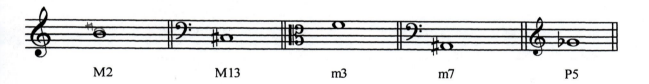

M2   M13   m3   m7   P5

A1   d3   m6   d12   P4

m9   A15   M7   A5   P8

Answers on page 143

Name: _____

Build the requested interval **below** the given note.

Example: Given: Answer:

            m3   m3

P5   A6   M3   d12   m3

P8   m6   M7   A2   A1

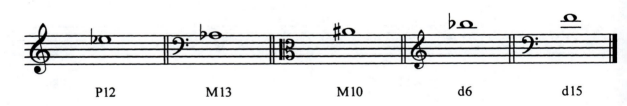

P12   M13   M10   d6   d15

Answers on page 144

ame: _____

Build the requested intervals **above** or **below** the given pitches, as specified.

Arrow pointing up = build interval above given pitch

Arrow pointing down = build interval below the given pitch

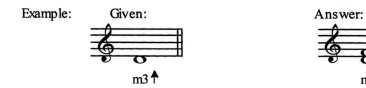

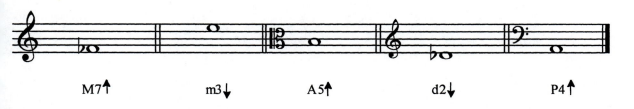

Answers on page 145

Name: _____

Identify the following intervals by **number** and **type**.

1. ____   2. ____   3. ____   4. ____   5. ____

6. ____   7. ____   8. ____   9. ____   10. ____

11. ____   12. ____   13. ____   14. ____   15. ____

Answers on page 146

Name: _____

Time limit: 15 minutes

Identify the given interval by **number** and **type**, then **write** and **identify** its inversion.

Example: Given: Answer:

M3   m6

Process: F-G-A = 1-2-3
F (tonic) to A (mediant) = M3
3 inverts to 6
M inverts to m

1. ____   2. ____   3. ____   4. ____   5. ____   6. ____

7. ____   8. ____   9. ____   10. ____   11. ____   12. ____

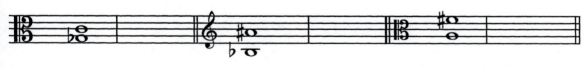

13. ____   14. ____   15. ____   16. ____   17. ____   18. ____

19. ____   20. ____

Answers on page 147

Name: _____   Time limit: 10 minutes

1. Identify the given interval by **number** and **type**, then **write** and **identify** its inversion.

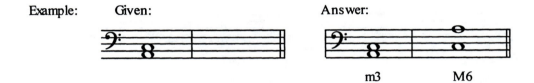

2. Build the requested intervals **above and below** the given pitches.

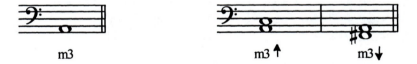

Answers on page 148

Identify the following intervals by **number**.

Example: Given: Answer:

_____   __3__

1. __2__   2. __6__   3. __5__   4. __3__   5. __7__

6. __4__   7. __8__   8. __4__   9. __2__   10. __2__

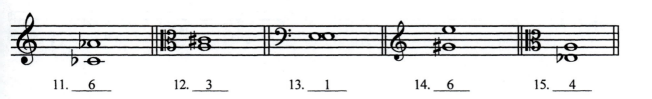

11. __6__   12. __3__   13. __1__   14. __6__   15. __4__

16. __6__   17. __4__   18. __8__   19. __3__   20. __6__

Identify the following intervals by **number** and **type**. All intervals will be either major or perfect.

Example: Given: Answer:

_____   P5

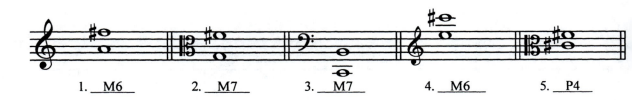

1. __M6__   2. __M7__   3. __M7__   4. __M6__   5. __P4__

6. __M6__   7. __M2__   8. __P5__   9. __P8__   10. __M3__

11. __P4__   12. __M3__   13. __M3__   14. __P8__   15. __P4__

Identify the following intervals by **number** and **type**. Be sure to determine the **number** first..

Example: Given: Answer:

                  ———   ___M3___

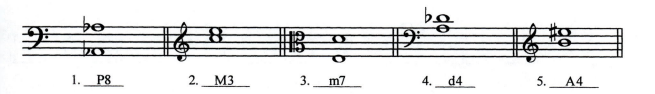

1. __P8__   2. __M3__   3. __m7__   4. __d4__   5. __A4__

6. __m2__   7. __M2__   8. __M6__   9. __P5__   10. __m6__

11. __A4__   12. __A6__   13. __m6__   14. __M3__   15. __P1__

16. __m6__   17. __d5__   18. __m2__   19. __P4__   20. __M7__

Identify the following intervals by **number** and **type**. Be sure to determine the **number** first.

Example: Given: Answer:

          _   _P5_

1. _d3_   2. _A7_   3. _d5_   4. _m6_   5. _d4_

6. _A8_   7. _d5_   8. _A5_   9. _A2_   10. _d5_

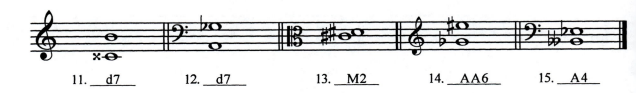

11. _d7_   12. _d7_   13. _M2_   14. _AA6_   15. _A4_

Build the requested interval **above** the given note.

Example: Given: Answer:

m3   m3

M2   M13   m3   m7   P5

A1   d3   m6   d12   P4

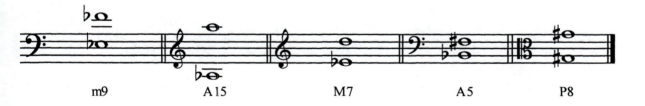

m9   A15   M7   A5   P8

Build the requested interval **below** the given note.

Example: Given: Answer:

           m3   m3

   P5   A6   M3   d12   m3

   P8   m6   M7   A2   A1

   P12   M13   M10   d6   d15

Build the requested intervals **above** or **below** the given pitches, as specified.

Arrow pointing up = build interval above given pitch

Arrow pointing down = build interval below the given pitch

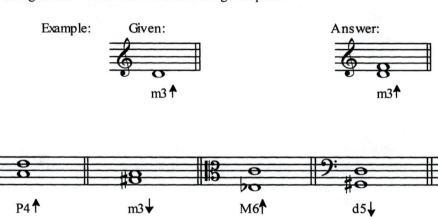

Identify the following intervals by **number** and **type**.

Example: Given: Answer:

M10

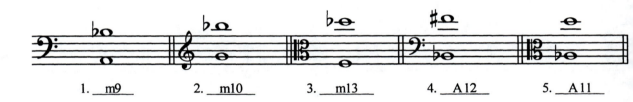

1. __m9__   2. __m10__   3. __m13__   4. __A12__   5. __A11__

6. __m9__   7. __d9__   8. __AA8__   9. __P11__   10. __m9__

11. __M10__   12. __d6__   13. __M14__   14. __A9__   15. __A15__

Identify the given interval by **number** and **type**, then **write** and **identify** its inversion.

Example: Given: Answer:

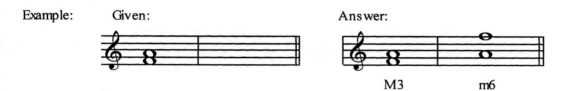

M3   m6

Process: F-G-A = 1-2-3
          F (tonic) to A (mediant) = M3
          3 inverts to 6
          M inverts to m

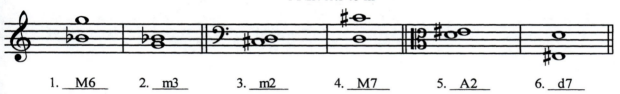

1. M6   2. m3   3. m2   4. M7   5. A2   6. d7

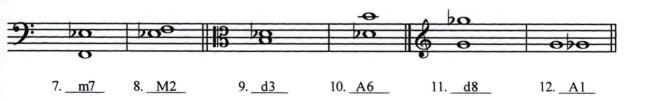

7. m7   8. M2   9. d3   10. A6   11. d8   12. A1

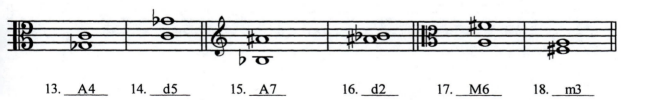

13. A4   14. d5   15. A7   16. d2   17. M6   18. m3

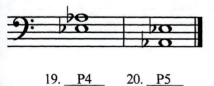

19. P4   20. P5

1. Identify the given interval by **number** and **type**, then **write** and **identify** its inversion.

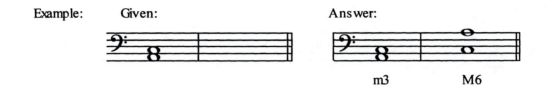

Example: Given: Answer:

m3   M6

P4   P5   m2   M7   A6   d3

2. Build the requested intervals **above and below** the given pitches.

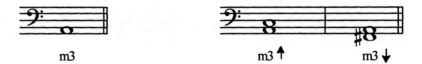

m3   m3 ↑   m3 ↓

P5 ↑   P5 ↓   M3 ↑   M3 ↓

m7 ↑   m7 ↓   A2 ↑   A2 ↓

NAME: _____

1. Identify the given interval by **number** and **type**, then **write** and **identify** its inversion. (3 points each)

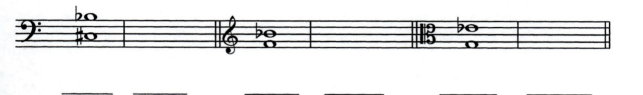

_____   _____   _____   _____   _____   _____

_____   _____   _____   _____

2. Build the requested intervals **above and below** the given pitches. (1 point each)

M6↑   M6↓   d3↑   d3↓   P8↑   P8↓

149

CHAPTER FIVE   Minor Scales

Most music of the common practice period is in major or minor keys. The minor scale is an abstraction that explains the pitch events that occur in compositions in minor keys.

1.   Scales and Scale Degrees

Most of the music you study and play is either major or minor. Yet students are traditionally taught that there are three distinct minor scales:

> natural or pure minor;
> harmonic minor; and
> melodic minor.

No one describes a piece as being in "E harmonic minor." We group all three forms of the minor scale under the simple rubric of "minor."

Each of the three forms of the minor scales has the same pattern of half and whole steps for its first five scale degrees. The differences are in their sixth and seventh scale degrees.

The names of the first five scale degrees are the same as in major scales: tonic, supertonic, mediant, subdominant, and dominant. Four of these pitches ($\hat{1}$, $\hat{2}$, $\hat{4}$, $\hat{5}$) are the same in major and minor scales that share the same tonic pitch. All major scales have a **major third** between the tonic and the mediant. All minor scales have a **minor third** between the tonic and the mediant.

D Major		D Minor
D	tonic	D
E	supertonic	E
F#	**mediant**	**F♮**
G	subdominant	G
A	dominant	A

Major and minor scales that have the same tonic, such as D major and D minor, are called **parallel** keys. The parallel major of D minor is D major; the parallel minor of D major is D minor.

> Drill: Going up and then down the circle of fifths, give alphabetic names for the first five notes in each major scale and its parallel minor (e.g., C major, C-D-E-F-G and C minor, C-D-E♭-F-G; G major, G-A-B-C-D and G minor, G-A-B♭-C-D). When you lower the mediant a half step, you must keep the same letter name: naturals become flats (E to E♭); sharps become naturals (A# to A♮); flats become double flats (B♭ to B♭♭).

Homework Assignment #1, p. 161

151

The natural, harmonic, and melodic forms of the minor scale all share the same tonic, supertonic, mediant, subdominant, and dominant notes. The sixth and seventh degrees vary according to the specific musical context.

2. Natural Minor Scale

The pattern of the natural minor scale includes five whole steps and two half steps in the following order: whole step, half step, whole step, whole step, half step, whole step, whole step.

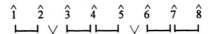

To build a natural minor scale above any note, simply follow the prescribed pattern.

Given: a   Answer: a

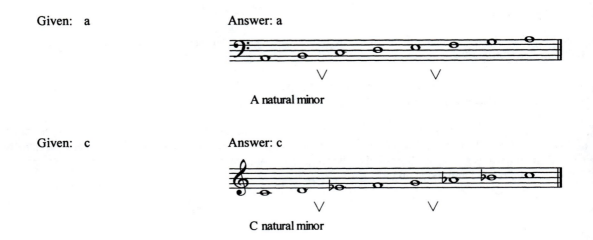

A natural minor

Given: c   Answer: c

C natural minor

The half step between $\hat{5}$ and $\hat{6}$ makes $\hat{6}$ pull toward $\hat{5}$. When $\hat{6}$ is a half step above $\hat{5}$, it is called the **lowered submediant.**

The whole step between $\hat{7}$ and $\hat{8}$ means that $\hat{7}$ does not pull toward $\hat{8}$. It is called the **subtonic**, not the leading tone.

All natural minor scales have a **minor sixth** between the tonic and the submediant. All natural minor scales have a **minor seventh** between the tonic and the subtonic.

The note names for the natural minor scale are:

$\hat{1}$ tonic
$\hat{2}$ supertonic
$\hat{3}$ mediant
$\hat{4}$ subdominant
$\hat{5}$ dominant
$\hat{6}$ **submediant** (sometimes called **lowered submediant**)   a half step above the dominant
$\hat{7}$ **subtonic**   a whole step below the tonic

Drill: Say the scale degrees and their proper names for the ascending and descending natural minor scale, clapping to keep a steady beat.

Homework Assignments #2 and #3, pp. 163-164

3.   Harmonic Minor Scale

The harmonic minor scale describes a compositional situation where the pull of the leading tone to the tonic is desirable for the melody and harmony. When the natural minor scale's seventh degree is altered so that it has a leading tone instead of a subtonic, the resulting scale is called a harmonic minor scale. It has a pattern of whole step, half step, whole step, whole step, half step, step-and-a-half, and half step.

$$\hat{1} \quad \hat{2} \quad \hat{3} \quad \hat{4} \quad \hat{5} \quad \hat{6} \quad \boxed{A2} \quad \hat{7} \quad \hat{8}$$

To build a harmonic minor scale above any note, think about the reason for its existence: to provide a leading tone to the tonic while retaining the minor third and minor sixth above the tonic.

The following harmonic minor scales are written to reflect the pattern commonly found in Western music of the common practice period: $\hat{6}$ pulls to $\hat{5}$, $\hat{7}$ pulls to $\hat{8}$ ($\hat{1}$).

D harmonic minor

F# harmonic minor

It is conventional to arrange scales so that their degrees are strictly ascending and descending ($\hat{1}$ - $\hat{2}$ - $\hat{3}$ - $\hat{4}$ - $\hat{5}$ - $\hat{6}$ - $\hat{7}$ - $\hat{8}$ and $\hat{8}$ - $\hat{7}$ - $\hat{6}$ - $\hat{5}$ - $\hat{4}$ - $\hat{3}$ - $\hat{2}$ - $\hat{1}$). If the notes of the harmonic scale were arranged in this fashion, the result would be an interval of an augmented second between $\hat{6}$ and $\hat{7}$.

Conventional arrangement of D harmonic minor

The augmented second is not a step or half step and is therefore outside the traditional definition of a scale (a succession of steps and/or half steps). The augmented second divides the melody into two distinct parts and is therefore not a melodically graceful interval. The augmented second is uncommon in the music of the common practice period, except when it is used for expressive purposes.

The note names for the harmonic minor scale are:

$\hat{1}$ tonic
$\hat{2}$ supertonic
$\hat{3}$ mediant
$\hat{4}$ subdominant
$\hat{5}$ dominant
$\hat{6}$ **lowered submediant**   a half step above the dominant
$\hat{7}$ **leading tone**   a half step below the tonic

Drill: Say the scale degrees and their proper names for the ascending and descending harmonic minor scale, clapping to keep a steady beat.

Homework Assignments #4 and #5, pp. 165-167

4.   Melodic Minor Scale

The melodic minor scale is the only common Western scale that has one set of notes going up and another set coming down. The melodic minor scale, ascending, describes a compositional situation where the pull of the leading tone to the tonic is desirable for the melody and harmony, and a smooth melodic line is desired between the dominant and tonic notes. To avoid the augmented second between $\hat{6}$ and $\hat{7}$, the ascending melodic minor scale raises the submediant a half step (so that it is a major sixth rather than a minor sixth above tonic) and raises the subtonic to a leading tone (as in the harmonic minor).

$\hat{1}$ $\hat{2}$ $\hat{3}$ $\hat{4}$ $\hat{5}$ $\natural\hat{6}$ $\hat{7}$ $\hat{8}$

The ascending melodic minor scale has a pattern of five whole steps, and two half steps, just like the major scale. The ascending melodic minor scale has half steps between $\hat{2}$ and $\hat{3}$, and $\hat{7}$ and $\hat{8}$; the major scale has half steps between $\hat{3}$ and $\hat{4}$, and $\hat{7}$ and $\hat{8}$.

154

To build an ascending melodic minor scale above any note, think about the reason for its existence: to provide a smooth melodic line (a series of steps and half steps between the dominant and the tonic). It does this by raising 6 and 7 by a half step each.

D melodic minor, ascending

F# melodic minor, ascending

The descending melodic minor scale, because it is not trying to pull toward the upper tonic, does not need the altered 6̂ and 7̂ degrees. In fact, the half step between 6̂ and 5̂ strengthens the importance of the dominant. The descending melodic minor scale uses the subtonic and lowered submediant, which lead smoothly (by step and half step) to the dominant. The subtonic or flat seventh scale degree is a half step lower than the leading tone; therefore, if the leading tone is a sharped pitch, the subtonic is a natural pitch; if the leading tone is a natural pitch, the subtonic is a flat pitch. The descending melodic minor scale is the same as the natural minor scale.

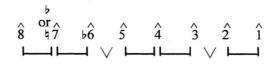

D melodic minor, descending

F# melodic minor, descending

To build a melodic minor scale starting on any pitch, think about making a smooth melodic line of steps and half steps between 5̂ and 8̂ that pushes the scale toward the tonic on the way up and the dominant on the way down.

155

The note names for the melodic minor scale are:

Ascending

$\hat{1}$ tonic
$\hat{2}$ supertonic
$\hat{3}$ mediant
$\hat{4}$ subdominant
$\hat{5}$ dominant
$\hat{6}$ **raised** submediant   a whole step above the dominant and a whole step below the leading tone
$\hat{7}$ **leading tone**   a half step below the tonic
$\hat{8}$ tonic

Descending

$\hat{8}$ tonic
$\hat{7}$ **subtonic**   a whole step below the tonic
$\hat{6}$ **lowered submediant**   a whole step below the subtonic and a half step above the dominant
$\hat{5}$ dominant
$\hat{4}$ subdominant
$\hat{3}$ mediant
$\hat{2}$ supertonic
$\hat{1}$ tonic

Drill: Say the scale degrees and their proper names for the ascending and descending melodic minor scale, clapping to keep a steady beat.

Homework Assignments #6 and #7, pp. 168-170

5.   Key Signatures

The key signatures for minor keys are derived similarly to those for major keys. They reflect the accidentals that occur in the **natural** minor scale. Alterations in the harmonic and melodic minor scales are made individually for each affected scale degree.

As in major keys, the order of these collected accidentals is by perfect fifth. Sharps are added by ascending perfect fifth; flats are added by descending perfect fifth.

Any minor keys whose tonics are related by perfect fifth have six notes that are the same and one that is different.

	$\hat{1}$	$\hat{2}$	$\hat{3}$	$\hat{4}$	$\hat{5}$	$\flat\hat{6}$	$\hat{7}$	$\hat{8}$
G minor:	G	A	B♭	C	D	E♭	F	G

	$\hat{4}$	$\hat{5}$	$\flat\hat{6}$	$\hat{7}$	$\hat{8}$ $(\hat{1})$	$\hat{2}$	$\hat{3}$	$\hat{4}$
D minor:	G	A	B♭	C	D	E	F	G

156

The circle of fifths is as convenient for minor keys as for major keys.

Three pairs of keys are shown overlapping at the bottom of the circle. These pairs are enharmonic equivalents of each other: they sound the same but are notated differently.

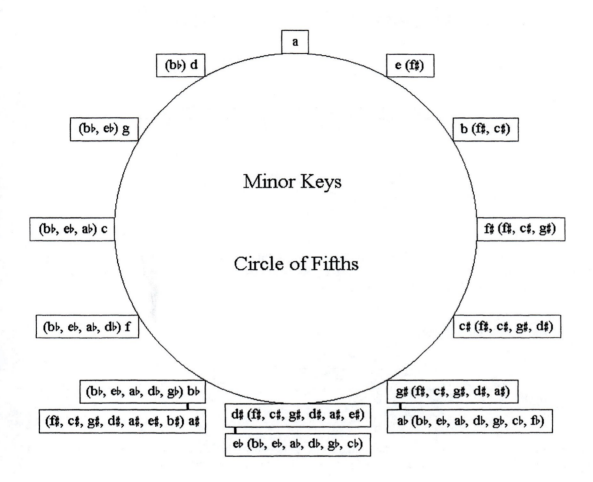

Drill: Practice saying ascending fifths aloud while looking at the chart, and then looking away. Clap to maintain a steady beat.

Drill: Practice saying descending fifths aloud while looking at the chart, and then looking away. Clap to maintain a steady beat.

Homework Assignment #8, p. 171

6.   Relative Major and Minor Scales

Major and minor scales that *share the same key signature* are called **relative** scales.

G: $\hat{1}$ $\hat{2}$ $\hat{3}$ $\hat{4}$ $\hat{5}$ $\hat{6}$ $\hat{7}$ $\hat{1}$

e: $\hat{3}$ $\hat{4}$ $\hat{5}$ $\hat{6}$ $\hat{7}$ $\hat{1}$ $\hat{2}$ $\hat{3}$

Key signature of 1 sharp (F#): G major and E minor
G major is the relative major of E minor.
E minor is the relative minor of G major.

To find the **relative minor** of a major scale, go to the note a **minor third below the tonic** (three half steps). You must be careful to use the letter name that is a third below. Another way to find the **relative minor** of a major scale is to name the **submediant** of the major scale.

Relative minor of D major:

D   b

A minor third below D is B (D-C#-C-B, three half steps; going down the D major scale, the third note is B, a minor third below tonic; the submediant, $\hat{6}$, of D major is B). The relative minor of D major is B minor.

Relative minor of E♭ major:

E♭   c

A minor third below E♭ is C (E♭-D-D♭-C, three half steps; going down the E♭ major scale, the third note is C, a minor third below tonic; the submediant, $\hat{6}$, of the E♭ major scale is C). The relative minor of E♭ major is C minor.

158

To find the **relative major** of a minor scale, go to the note a **minor third above the tonic** (three half steps). You must go to a letter name a third above as well. Another way to find the relative major of a minor scale is to find **mediant**, $\hat{3}$, of the minor scale.

Relative major of E minor:

A minor third above E is G (E-F-F#-G, three half steps; the mediant of E minor is G; in E major, $\hat{3}$ is G#, which is a major third; therefore E to G is a minor third).

Relative major of F minor:

A minor third above F is A♭ (F-F#-G-A♭, three half steps; the mediant of F minor is A♭; in F major, $\hat{3}$ is A, which is a major third; therefore F to A♭ is a minor third).

The circle of fifths shows the pairs of relative major and minor keys.

Three pairs of keys are shown overlapping at the bottom of the circle. These pairs are enharmonic equivalents of each other: they sound the same but are notated differently.

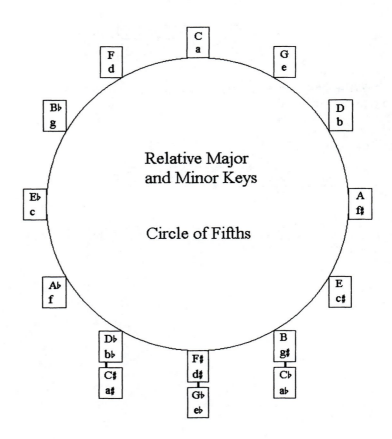

Drill: Beginning with C major and A minor, move up and then down the circle naming all major and minor keys and their key signatures (C major, A minor, no sharps or flats; G major, E minor, F#; D major, B minor, F#-C#; and so on).

Homework Assignments #9, #10, #11, and #12, pp. 172-175

Drill: Examine the beginnings of the following movements from Beethoven's String Quartets to identify their keys: pages (1) 1; (8) 8; (13) 13; (25) 1; (49) 7; 12 (54); (65) 1; 14 (78); (83) 1; (103) 1; (109) 7. Look carefully at the key signatures *and* at the notes. If the piece is in minor, you will probably find the leading tone in the first or second measure; you will also find the appropriate tonic and dominant notes in the first or second measure.

PRACTICE QUIZ ON CHAPTER FIVE, p. 176

Name: _____

On the staves provided, write out the **first five notes** of the requested **parallel** scales, using half notes. Do not use key signatures. Label each example as shown below.

Example: Given: C major
C minor

Answer:

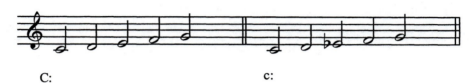

C: c:

1. F major and F minor, treble clef

2. B major and B minor, bass clef

3. A major and A minor, treble clef

4. G major and G minor, bass clef

5. E major and E minor, alto clef

6. C♯ major and C♯ minor, treble clef

7. B♭ major and B♭ minor, bass clef

8. F♯ major and F♯ minor, alto clef

9. A♭ major and A♭ minor, treble clef

Answers on pages 177-178

Name: _____

Time limit: 10 minutes

On the staves provided, write out the requested **natural minor scales** in the given clefs, using half notes. Indicate all half steps. **Do not use key signatures.**

Example: Given: B natural minor, treble clef

Answer:

b:

1. D natural minor, bass clef

5. F natural minor, treble clef

2. A♯ natural minor, bass clef

6. F♯ natural minor, treble clef

3. G natural minor, alto clef

7. E natural minor, bass clef

4. B♭ natural minor, treble clef

8. C♯ natural minor, alto clef

Answers on page 179

Name: _____

Without referring to a written chart, fill in the blanks in the following sentences with the correct answers for the **natural minor scale**.

    Example: Question: The tonic is _____.

                   Answer: The tonic is __$\hat{1}$__.

1. The submediant is _____.

2. The subtonic is _____.

3. The supertonic is _____.

4. The dominant is _____.

5. The mediant is _____.

6. The subdominant is _____.

Without referring to a written chart, fill in the blanks in the following sentences with the correct answers for the **natural minor scale**.

    Example: Question: $\hat{1}$ is called the _____.

                   Answer: $\hat{1}$ is called the _tonic_.

1. $\hat{3}$ is called the _____.

2. $\hat{6}$ is called the _____.

3. $\hat{4}$ is called the _____.

4. $\hat{7}$ is called the _____.

5. $\hat{2}$ is called the _____.

6. $\hat{5}$ is called the _____.

Answers on page 180

Name: _____

Time limit: 15 minutes

On the staves provided, write out the requested **harmonic minor scales** in the given clefs, using half notes. Indicate all half steps. **Do not use key signatures**.

Example: Given: B harmonic minor, treble clef

Answer:

b:

1. A harmonic minor, bass clef

2. E♭ harmonic minor, treble clef

3. C harmonic minor, bass clef

4. E harmonic minor, treble clef

HOMEWORK ASSIGNMENT #4
(continued)

5. F harmonic minor, alto clef

6. C♯ harmonic minor, bass clef

7. A♭ harmonic minor, treble clef

8. G harmonic minor, alto clef

Answers on pages 181-182

Name: _____

Without referring to a written chart, fill in the blanks in the following sentences with the correct answers for the **harmonic minor scale**.

    Example: Question: The tonic is _____.

                        Answer: The tonic is __$\hat{1}$__.

1.   The dominant is _____.

2.   The mediant is _____.

3.   The supertonic is _____.

4.   The lowered submediant is _____.

5.   The subdominant is _____.

6.   The leading tone is _____.

Without referring to a written chart, fill in the blanks in the following sentences with the correct answers for the **harmonic minor scale**.

    Example: Question: $\hat{1}$ is called the _____.

                        Answer: $\hat{1}$ is called the _tonic_.

1. $\hat{6}$ is called the _____.

2. $\hat{2}$ is called the _____.

3. $\hat{4}$ is called the _____.

4. $\hat{7}$ is called the _____.

5. $\hat{3}$ is called the _____.

6. $\hat{5}$ is called the _____.

Answers on page 183

Name:_____   Time limit: 15 minutes

On the staves provided, write out the requested **melodic minor scales, ascending AND descending**, in the given clefs, using half notes. Indicate all half steps. **Do not use key signatures**.

Example: Given: B melodic minor, bass clef

            Answer:

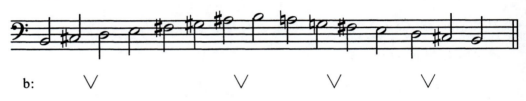

            b:

1. E melodic minor, alto clef

2. G melodic minor, treble clef

3. F♯ melodic minor, bass clef

4. F melodic minor, treble clef

HOMEWORK ASSIGNMENT #6
(continued)

5. G♯ melodic minor, alto clef

6. D melodic minor, bass clef

7. A melodic minor, treble clef

8. C♯ melodic minor, alto clef

Answers on pages 184-185

Name: _____   Time limit: 5 minutes

Without referring to a written chart, fill in the blanks in the following sentences with the correct answers for the **melodic minor scale**.

        Example: Question: The tonic is _____.

                       Answer: The tonic is ___$\hat{1}$___.

1.   The dominant is _____.

2.   The mediant is _____.

3.   The supertonic is _____.

4.   The lowered submediant is _____ in the melodic _____ scale.

5.   The leading tone is _____ in the melodic _____ scale.

6.   The leading tone is _____ in the melodic _____ scale.

7.   The subdominant is _____.

8.   The raised submediant is _____ in the melodic _____ scale.

Without referring to a written chart, fill in the blanks in the following sentences with the correct answers for the **melodic minor scale**.

        Example: Question: $\hat{1}$ is called the _____.

                       Answer: $\hat{1}$ is called the _tonic_.

1. $\hat{6}$ is called the _____ in the melodic **ascending** scale.

2. $\hat{4}$ is called the _____.

3. $\hat{2}$ is called the _____.

4. $\hat{7}$ is called the _____ in the melodic **descending** scale.

5. $\hat{6}$ is called the _____ in the melodic **ascending** scale.

6. $\hat{3}$ is called the _____.

7. $\hat{5}$ is called the _____.

8. $\hat{7}$ is called the _____ in the melodic **ascending** scale.

Answers on page 186

For every pitch listed below, name the notes a perfect fifth above and below.

Given: _____ C _____

Answer: _____ F   C   G _____

1. _____ B♭ _____   5. _____ A _____

2. _____ C# _____   6. _____ F# _____

3. _____ D♭ _____   7. _____ E _____

4. _____ G _____   8. _____ B _____

For every minor key listed below, name the minor keys a perfect fifth above and below.

Given: _____ C minor _____

Answer: _____ F minor   C minor   G minor _____

1. _____ B minor _____

2. _____ D minor _____

3. _____ B♭ minor _____

4. _____ G# minor _____

5. _____ F minor _____

6. _____ E♭ minor _____

7. _____ D# minor _____

Answers on page 187

Name: _____

Time limit: 15 minutes

On the staff provided, write the requested key signature in the proper clef. Write the tonic note of the scale as a half note.

Example: Given: C minor, bass clef

Answer:

c:

1. E minor, treble clef

2. G minor, alto clef

3. F♯ minor, bass clef

4. A♭ minor, treble clef

5. C♯ minor, bass clef

6. D minor, alto clef

7. B minor, treble clef

8. F minor, bass clef

9. D♯ minor, treble clef

Answers on page 188

ame: _____   Time limit: 10 minutes

Fill in the blanks below.

      Example: Question: The relative major of D minor is _____.

                       Answer: The relative major of D minor is _____F major_____.

1. The relative minor of C# major is_____.

2. The parallel major of D minor is _____.

3. The parallel minor of F# major is _____.

4. The relative major of E minor is _____.

5. The parallel minor of A♭ major is _____.

6. The relative minor of B major is _____.

7. The relative minor of D♭ major is_____.

8. The relative minor of B♭ major is _____.

9. The parallel minor of E major is _____.

10. The parallel major of G minor is _____.

11. The relative minor of E♭ major is _____.

12. The relative major of F minor is _____.

13. The relative major of B♭ minor is _____.

14. The parallel minor of B♭ major is _____.

Answers on page 189

Name: _____

Time limit: 10 minutes

Name the major **and** minor keys represented by the following key signatures.

Example: Given: Answer:

                    ___B♭, c___

 _____

 _____

 _____

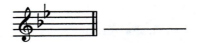 _____

 _____

 _____

 _____

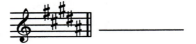 _____

 _____

 _____

 _____

 _____

 _____

Answers on page 190

ame: _____   Time limit: 10 minutes

Fill in the blanks in the sentences below.

     Example: Question: The supertonic of E minor is _____.

                     Answer: The supertonic of E minor is _____ F# _____.

1. The lowered submediant of F minor is _____.

2. The leading tone of A minor is _____.

3. The mediant of C# minor is _____.

4. The subtonic of A♭ minor is _____.

5. The dominant of G minor is _____.

6. The raised submediant of F# minor is _____.

7. The subdominant of G# minor is _____.

8. The lowered submediant of D minor is _____.

9. The leading tone of B♭ minor is _____.

10. The subtonic of B minor is _____.

11. The raised submediant of A# minor is _____.

12. The mediant of F minor is _____.

13. The lowered submediant of E minor is _____.

14. The leading tone of G# minor is _____.

15. The mediant of D minor is _____.

16. The dominant of B♭ minor is _____.

17. The lowered submediant of F# minor is _____.

18. The subtonic of C# minor is _____.

19. The supertonic of A# minor is _____.

20. The raised submediant of F minor is _____.

Answers on page 191

Name: _____

1. Write the requested minor scales in the given clef, one octave ascending **and** descending.

B harmonic minor

C melodic minor

2. Fill in the blanks below.

    a. The relative major of F minor is _____.

    b. The parallel minor of A major is _____.

    c. The relative minor of B major is _____.

    d. The lowered submediant of D minor is _____.

    e. The subtonic of C# minor is _____.

    f. The mediant of G minor is _____.

    g. The raised submediant of F# minor is _____.

    h. The leading tone of E minor is _____.

3. Name the **major** and **minor** keys represented by the following key signatures.

    _____   _____   _____

    _____   _____   _____

Answers on page 192

On the staves provided, write out the **first five notes** of the requested **parallel** scales, using half notes. Do not use key signatures. Label each example as shown below.

Example: Given: C Major
                                  C minor

                    Answer:

C: c:

1. F major and F minor, treble clef

F: f:

2. B major and B minor, bass clef

B: b:

3. A major and A minor, treble clef

A: a:

4. G major and G minor, bass clef

G: g:

HOMEWORK ANSWERS #1
(continued)

5. E major and E minor, alto clef

E: e:

6. C♯ major and C♯ minor, treble clef

C♯:   c♯:

7. E♭ major and E♭ minor, bass clef

E♭:   e♭:

8. F♯ major and F♯ minor, alto clef

F♯:   f♯:

9. A♭ major and A♭ minor, treble clef

A♭:   a♭:

178

On the staves provided, write out the requested **natural minor scales** in the given clefs, using half notes. Indicate all half steps. **Do not use key signatures.**

Example: Given: B natural minor, treble clef

Answer:

1. D natural minor, bass clef   5. F natural minor, treble clef

2. A♯ natural minor, bass clef   6. F♯ natural minor, treble clef

3. G natural minor, alto clef   7. E natural minor, bass clef

4. B♭ natural minor, treble clef   8. C♯ natural minor, alto clef

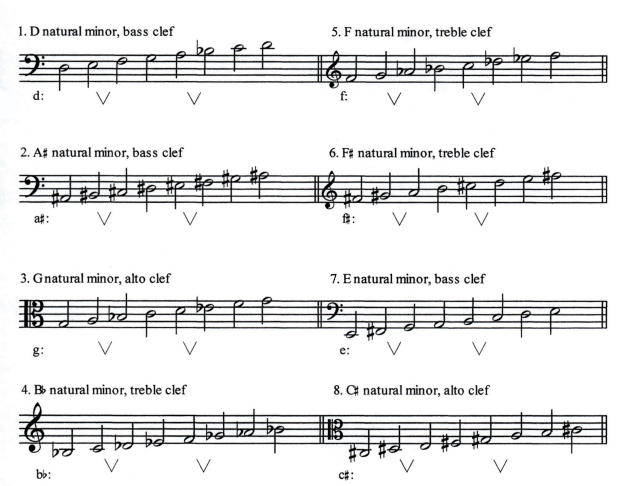

Without referring to a written chart, fill in the blanks in the following sentences with the correct answers for the **natural minor scale**.

Example: Question: The tonic is _____.

                Answer: The tonic is ___$\hat{1}$___.

1. The submediant is ___$\hat{6}$___.

2. The subtonic is ___$\hat{7}$___.

3. The supertonic is ___$\hat{2}$___.

4. The dominant is ___$\hat{5}$___.

5. The mediant is ___$\hat{3}$___.

6. The subdominant is ___$\hat{4}$___.

Without referring to a written chart, fill in the blanks in the following sentences with the correct answers for the **natural minor scale**.

Example: Question: $\hat{1}$ is called the _____.

                Answer: $\hat{1}$ is called the _tonic_.

1. $\hat{3}$ is called the _____mediant_____.

2. $\hat{6}$ is called the _____submediant_____.

3. $\hat{4}$ is called the _____subdominant_____.

4. $\hat{7}$ is called the _____subtonic_____.

5. $\hat{2}$ is called the _____supertonic_____.

6. $\hat{5}$ is called the _____dominant_____.

On the staves provided, write out the requested **harmonic minor scales** in the given clefs, using half notes. Indicate all half steps. **Do not use key signatures**.

Example: Given: B harmonic minor, treble clef

                         Answer:

1. A harmonic minor, bass clef

2. E♭ harmonic minor, treble clef

3. C harmonic minor, bass clef

4. E harmonic minor, treble clef

HOMEWORK ANSWERS #4
(continued)

5. F harmonic minor, alto clef

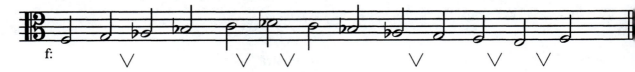

f:

6. C# harmonic minor, bass clef

c#:

7. A♭ harmonic minor, treble clef

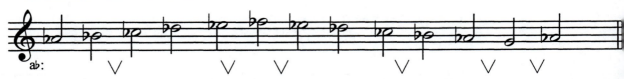

a♭:

8. G harmonic minor, alto clef

g:

Without referring to a written chart, fill in the blanks in the following sentences with the correct answers for the **harmonic minor scale**.

        Example: Question: The tonic is _____.

                            Answer: The tonic is ___$\hat{1}$___.

1. The dominant is ___$\hat{5}$___.

2. The mediant is ___$\hat{3}$___.

3. The supertonic is ___$\hat{2}$___.

4. The lowered submediant is ___$\hat{6}$___.

5. The subdominant is ___$\hat{4}$___.

6. The leading tone is ___$\hat{7}$___.

Without referring to a written chart, fill in the blanks in the following sentences with the correct answers for the **harmonic minor scale**.

        Example: Question: $\hat{1}$ is called the _____.

                            Answer: $\hat{1}$ is called the _tonic_.

1. $\hat{6}$ is called the _lowered submediant_.

2. $\hat{2}$ is called the _supertonic_.

3. $\hat{4}$ is called the _subdominant_.

4. $\hat{7}$ is called the _leading tone_.

5. $\hat{3}$ is called the _mediant_.

6. $\hat{5}$ is called the _dominant_.

On the staves provided, write out the requested **melodic minor scales, ascending AND descending**, in the given clefs, using half notes. Indicate all half steps. **Do not use key signatures**.

Example: Given: B melodic minor, bass clef

Answer:

b:

1. E melodic minor, alto clef

e:

2. G melodic minor, treble clef

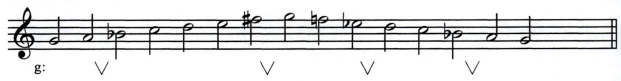

g:

3. F♯ melodic minor, bass clef

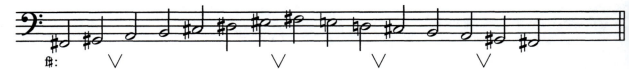

f♯:

4. F melodic minor, treble clef

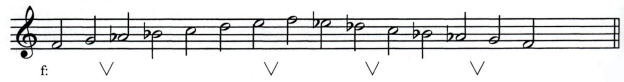

f:

HOMEWORK ANSWERS #6
(continued)

5. G# melodic minor, alto clef

6. D melodic minor, bass clef

7. A melodic minor, treble clef

8. C# melodic minor, alto clef

Without referring to a written chart, fill in the blanks in the following sentences with the correct answers for the **melodic minor scale**.

        Example: Question: The tonic is _____.

                           Answer: The tonic is __$\hat{1}$__.

1. The dominant is ___$\hat{5}$___.

2. The mediant is ___$\hat{3}$___.

3. The supertonic is ___$\hat{2}$___.

4. The lowered submediant is ___$\hat{6}$___ in the melodic _descending_ scale.

5. The leading tone is ___$\hat{7}$___ in the melodic _ascending_ scale.

6. The leading tone is ___$\hat{7}$___ in the melodic _ascending_ scale.

7. The subdominant is ___$\hat{4}$___.

8. The raised submediant is ___$\hat{6}$___ in the melodic _ascending_ scale.

Without referring to a written chart, fill in the blanks in the following sentences with the correct answers for the **melodic minor scale**.

        Example: Question: $\hat{1}$ is called the _____.

                           Answer: $\hat{1}$ is called the _tonic_.

1. $\hat{6}$ is called the ___raised submediant___ in the melodic **ascending** scale.

2. $\hat{4}$ is called the ___subdominant___.

3. $\hat{2}$ is called the ___supertonic___.

4. $\hat{7}$ is called the ___subtonic___ in the melodic **descending** scale.

5. $\hat{6}$ is called the ___raised submediant___ in the melodic **ascending** scale.

6. $\hat{3}$ is called the ___mediant___.

7. $\hat{5}$ is called the ___dominant___.

8. $\hat{7}$ is called the ___leading tone___ in the melodic **ascending** scale.

For every pitch listed below, name the notes a perfect fifth above and below.

Given: _____ C _____

Answer: ___ F   C   G ___

1.	Eb	Bb	F		5.	D	A	E
2.	F#	C#	G#		6.	B	F#	C#
3.	Gb	Db	Ab		7.	A	E	B
4.	C	G	D		8.	E	B	F#

For every minor key listed below, name the minor keys a perfect fifth above and below.

Given: _____ C minor _____

Answer: ___ F minor   C minor   G minor ___

1.	E minor	B minor	F# minor
2.	G minor	D minor	A minor
3.	Eb minor	Bb minor	F minor
4.	C# minor	G# minor	D# minor
5.	Bb minor	F minor	C minor
6.	Ab minor	Eb minor	Bb minor
7.	G# minor	D# minor	A# minor

On the staff provided, write the requested key signature in the proper clef. Write the tonic note of the scale as a half note.

Example: Given: C minor, bass clef

Answer:

Fill in the blanks below.

    Example: Question: The relative major of D minor is _____.

                    Answer: The relative major of D minor is _____F major_____.

1. The relative minor of C# major is_____A# minor_____.

2. The parallel major of D minor is _____D major_____.

3. The parallel minor of F# major is _____F# minor_____.

4. The relative major of E minor is _____G major_____.

5. The parallel minor of A♭ major is _____A♭ minor_____.

6. The relative minor of B major is _____G# minor_____.

7. The relative minor of D♭ major is_____B♭ minor_____.

8. The relative minor of B♭ major is _____G minor_____.

9. The parallel minor of E major is _____E minor_____.

10. The parallel major of G minor is _____G major_____.

11. The relative minor of E♭ major is _____C minor_____.

12. The relative major of F minor is _____A♭ major_____.

13. The relative major of B♭ minor is _____D♭ major_____.

14. The parallel minor of B♭ major is _____B♭ minor_____.

189

Name the major **and** minor keys represented by the following key signatures.

Example: Given: Answer:

_B♭, c_

_G, e_   _C, a_

_A♭, f_   _B♭, g_

_G♭, e♭_   _C♭, a♭_

_A, f♯_   _B♭, c_

_D♭, b♭_   _B, g♯_

_D, b_   _C♯, a♯_

_E, c♯_   _D, b_

_F, d_

Fill in the blanks in the sentences below.

      Example: Question: The supertonic of E minor is _____.

                          Answer: The supertonic of E minor is _____ F# _____.

1.   The lowered submediant of F minor is _____ D♭ _____.

2.   The leading tone of A minor is _____ G# _____.

3.   The mediant of C# minor is _____ E _____.

4.   The subtonic of A♭ minor is _____ G♭ _____.

5.   The dominant of G minor is _____ D _____.

6.   The raised submediant of F# minor is _____ D _____.

7.   The subdominant of G# minor is _____ C# ____.

8.   The lowered submediant of D minor is _____ B♭ _____.

9.   The leading tone of B♭ minor is _____ A _____.

10. The subtonic of B minor is ___ A ___.

11. The raised submediant of A# minor is _____ F✕ _____.

12. The mediant of F minor is ___ A♭ ___.

13. The lowered submediant of E minor is _____ C _____.

14. The leading tone of G# minor is_____ F✕ ___.

15. The mediant of D minor is _____ F _____.

16. The dominant of B♭ minor is_____ F _____.

17. The lowered submediant of F# minor is _____ D _____.

18. The subtonic of C# minor is _____ B _____.

19. The supertonic of A# minor is ____ B# _____.

20. The raised submediant of F minor is___ D ___.

1.   Write the requested minor scales in the given clef, one octave ascending **and** descending.

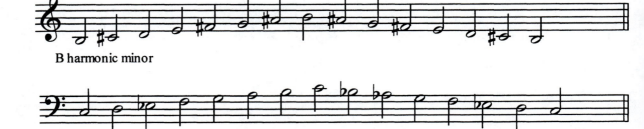

   B harmonic minor

   C melodic minor

2.   Fill in the blanks below.

      a. The relative major of F minor is _____ A major _____.

      b. The parallel minor of A major is _____ A minor _____.

      c. The relative minor of B major is _____ G# minor _____.

      d. The lowered submediant of D minor is ___ B♭ _____.

      e. The subtonic of C# minor is _____ B _____.

      f. The mediant of G minor is _____ B♭ _____.

      g. The raised submediant of F# minor is _____ D# _____.

      h. The leading tone of E minor is _____ D# _____.

3.   Name the **major** and **minor** keys represented by the following key signatures.

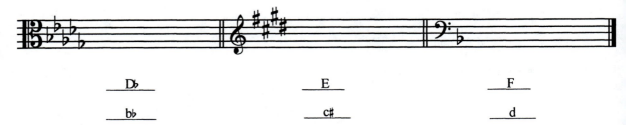

        _____ D♭ _____   _ E _   _ F _

        _____ b♭ _____   _ c# _   _ d _

NAME: _____

1. Write the requested minor scales in the given clef, one octave ascending **and** descending.
    (4 points each)

    F# harmonic minor

    D melodic minor

2. Fill in the blanks. (2 points each)

       a. The subtonic of F minor is _____.

       b. The relative major of G minor is _____.

       c. The raised submediant of E minor is _____.

       d. The parallel minor of B♭ major is _____.

       e. The mediant of E♭ minor is _____.

       f. The relative major of C# minor is _____.

       g. The leading tone of B minor is _____.

       h. The raised submediant of C minor is _____.

3. Name the **major** and **minor** keys represented by the following key signatures. (2 points each)

      _____   _____   _____

      _____   _____   _____

CHAPTER SIX   Triads

Western music's development has focused largely on harmony, the simultaneous sounding of three or more pitches, called chords.

1.   Root-Position Triads

A triad is a three-note collection of pitches (a chord) built by stacking major or minor thirds. The functional names for the notes in a triad are root (R), third (3), and fifth (5). Triads that appear as two consecutive thirds are called root-position triads.

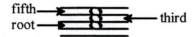

A triad is in **root position** when its **root** is the lowest sounding pitch.

Triads built from the root up always occupy three lines or three spaces on the staff.

Drill: Build root-position triads *above* the following notes by adding two thirds.

roots

Drill: Build root-position triads *below* the following notes by adding two thirds.

fifths

Drill: Build root-position triads using the following notes as the middle note in the triad (add one third above and one third below the given note).

thirds

Drill: Say the letter names for the triads that occur starting on every letter name (A, B, C, D, E, F, and G), beginning with A: A-C-E/E-C-A; B-D-F/F-D-B; C-E-G/G-E-C; D-F-A/A-F-D, and so on.

2.   Triad Types in Root Position

There are four types of triads: **major, minor, augmented,** and **diminished**. Triad type is determined by the quality of thirds and fifths in the triad.

A **major triad** has a major third between its root and third and a perfect fifth between its root and fifth. (A major third plus a minor third.)

A major triad is equivalent to the tonic ($\hat{1}$), mediant ($\hat{3}$) and dominant ($\hat{5}$) of a major key.

Drill: Using your knowledge of major scales, spell major triads on the tonic note of each of the major scales in the circle of fifths: C, G, D, A, E, B, F#, C#, F, B♭, E♭, A♭, D♭, G♭, and C♭. Spell the major triads ascending and descending. (C major: C-E-G/G-E-C; G major: G-B-D/D-B-G; D major: D-F#-A/A-F#-D; and so on.)

A **minor triad** has a minor third between its root and third and a perfect fifth between its root and fifth. (A minor third plus a major third.)

A minor triad is equivalent to the tonic ($\hat{1}$), mediant ($\hat{3}$) and dominant ($\hat{5}$) of a minor key.

Drill: Using your knowledge of minor scales, spell minor triads on the tonic note of each of the minor scales in the circle of fifths: a, e, b, f#, c#, g#, d#, a#, d, g, c, f, b♭, e♭, and a♭. Spell the minor triads ascending and descending. (A minor: a-c-e/e-c-a; E minor: e-g-b/b-g-e; B minor: b-d-f#/f#-d-b; and so on.)

An **augmented triad** has a major third between its root and third and an augmented fifth between its root and fifth. (A major third plus a major third.)

196

Drill: Using your knowledge of major thirds (4 half steps spanning three letter names or the tonic and mediant of a major scale), spell augmented triads on the tonic note of each of the major scales in the circle of fifths: C, G, D, A, E, B, F#, C#, F, Bb, Eb, Ab, Db, Gb, and Cb. Spell the augmented triads ascending and descending. (C major: C-E-G#/G#-E-C; G major: G-B-D#/D#-B-G; D major: D-F#-A#/A#-F#-D; and so on.) Augmented triads do not occur above the tonic of the major scale in common practice.

A **diminished triad** has a minor third between its root and third and a diminished fifth between its root and fifth.

Drill: Using your knowledge of minor thirds, spell diminished triads on the tonic note of each of the minor scales in the circle of fifths: a, e, b, f#, c#, g#, d#, a#, d, g, c, f, bb, eb, and ab. Spell the diminished triads ascending and descending. (A dim: a-c-eb/eb-c-a; E dim: e-g-bb/bb-g-e; B dim: b-d-f/f-d-b; etc.) Diminished triads do not naturally occur above the tonic of the minor scale.

Homework Assignment #1, p. 205

3.   Building Triads

To build any type of triad, determine the required root, third, and fifth; put the root on bottom and stack the third and fifth above it.

Given: Build a root-position minor triad with Ab as its root.

Answer:

Process: Ab to Cb is a minor third;
         Ab to Eb is a perfect fifth;
         in ab minor, the tonic, mediant, and dominant are Ab, Cb, and Eb, respectively;
         Ab is the root and must be the lowest pitch.

Given: Build a root-position major triad with D as its third.

Answer:

Process: If D is the third of the triad, the root will be some kind of B, and the fifth will
         be some kind of F.
         A minor third above D is F, and a major third below D is B♭.
         Also, B♭ to F is a perfect fifth.

Drill: Practice building major, minor, augmented, and diminished triads above every note in the C
         major and C minor scales; the D major and D minor scales; the E major and E minor scales; the
         F major and F minor scales; and so on.

Drill: Practice building major, minor, augmented and diminished triads using every white note and
         black note on the keyboard as the third of the triad. For example: if A is the third of a major
         triad, the triad is F-A-C; if A is the third of a minor triad, the triad is F#-A-C#; if A is the third
         of an augmented triad, the triad is F-A-C#; if A is the third of a diminished triad, the triad is F#-
         A-C. Continue using the white notes (B, C, D, E, F, and G) and the black notes (B♭, C#, D♭, E♭,
         F#, G♭, G#, and A♭).

Homework Assignment #2, p. 206

4.   First-Inversion and Second-Inversion Triads

All triads with their root written as the lowest note are root-position triads. These triads may be written in close
spacing (stacked thirds) or open spacing (same notes but not in stacked thirds).

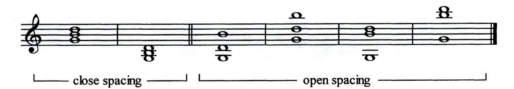

All root-position triads are called $^5_3$ chords because they contain a third and fifth above the bass note.

Drill: Write the given triads in open spacing.

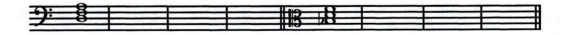

A triad is in **first inversion** when its **third** is the lowest note. All triads with their third written as the lowest pitch are first-inversion triads. These triads may be written in close or open spacing.

First-inversion triads are often called 6 chords (6 is short for $^6_3$) because they contain a sixth and a third above the bass note.

Drill: Write the given first-inversion triads in open spacing.

A triad is in **second inversion** when its **fifth** is the lowest pitch. All triads with their fifth written as the lowest pitch are second-inversion triads. These triads may be written in close or open spacing.

Second-inversion triads are often called $^6_4$ chords because they contain a sixth and a fourth above the bass.

Drill: Write the given second-inversion triads in open spacing.

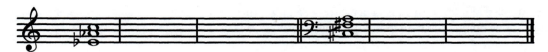

Homework Assignments #3, #4, and #5, pp. 207-209

5.   Identifying Root-Position, First- and Second-Inversion Triads

To determine the position of a triad, find the *root*. Arrange the three notes so they are in thirds and determine whether the root, third, or fifth is in the bass. This is most easily done by naming the pitches and arranging them into thirds. N.B.: Triads on consecutive lines or spaces are always in root position.

Given: Identify the chord position:

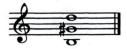

Answer: 6 chord

Process: Stack in thirds: G#-B-D;
therefore, G# = R, B = 3, D = 5.
Since B is the lowest note,
this is a first inversion (6) triad.

Homework Assignments #6 and #7, pp. 210-211

6.   Triads in the Major Scale

Scale degrees are indicated by arabic numerals with carets ($\hat{1}$, $\hat{2}$, $\hat{3}$, $\hat{4}$, $\hat{5}$, $\hat{6}$, $\hat{7}$ and $\hat{8}$).

Triads are indicated by roman numerals. Uppercase roman numerals indicate major triads (e.g., I); lowercase numerals indicate minor triads (e.g., ii); uppercase numerals with plus signs indicate augmented triads (e.g., III+); lowercase numerals with degree signs indicate diminished triads (e.g., vii°).

There are three major triads in a major scale: I, IV, and V. There are three minor triads in a major scale: ii, iii, and vi. There is one diminished triad in a major scale: vii°.

I   ii   iii   IV   V   vi   vii°

Drill: The following singing exercise will help you remember the triad types in the major scale:

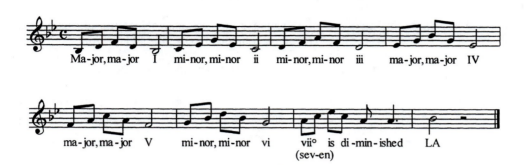

Ma-jor, ma-jor I   mi-nor, mi-nor ii   mi-nor, mi-nor iii   ma-jor, ma-jor IV

ma-jor, ma-jor V   mi-nor, mi-nor vi   vii° is di-min-ished   LA
(sev-en)

The triads in the major scale can be written in root position, first inversion, or second inversion. The quality of a triad (M, m, A or d) is not affected by which pitch is in the bass.

When writing first-inversion or second-inversion triads in a key, be sure to spell the correct root-third-fifth first, then put the correct pitch in the bass.

Drill: Using the major keys in the circle of fifths, spell the I, IV, and V chords (ascending and descending) in each key in root position. (C, G, D, A, E, B, F#, C#, F, B♭, E♭, A♭, D♭, G♭, C♭): C major: I is C-E-G/G-E-C, IV is F-A-C/C-A-F, V is G-B-D/D-B-G, and so on.

Drill: Using the major keys in the circle of fifths, spell the I⁶, IV⁶, and V⁶ chords (ascending and descending) in each key in close position. (C, G, D, A, E, B, F#, C#, F, B♭, E♭, A♭, D♭, G♭, C♭): C major: I is E-G-C/C-G-E, IV is A-C-F/F-C-A, V is B-D-G/G-D-B, and so on.

Homework Assignments #8 and #9, pp. 212-213

7.   Triads in the Minor Scale

Triads in the minor scale reflect two possibilities when the triad contains the sixth or seventh scale degree. Triads with $\hat{6}$ may occur with either the lowered submediant ($♭\hat{6}$) or the raised submediant ($♮\hat{6}$ or $♯\hat{6}$). Triads with $\hat{7}$ may contain either the subtonic ($♭\hat{7}$) or the leading tone ($♮\hat{7}$ or $♯\hat{7}$). While the major scale has only seven triads, the minor scale has thirteen possible triads. The most common forms of each triad are shown in whole notes, below. The less common forms of each triad with two possible forms are shown as stemless quarter notes.

i   ii°   (ii)   (III)   III+   iv   (IV)   (v)   V   VI   (vi°)   (VII)   vii°

There are five major triads in minor scales: III (natural minor and descending melodic minor); IV (ascending melodic minor); V (harmonic minor and ascending melodic minor); VI (natural minor and descending melodic minor); and VII (natural minor and descending melodic minor).

201

There are four minor triads in minor scales: i (all minor scales); ii (ascending melodic minor); iv (natural minor, harmonic minor and descending melodic minor); and v (natural minor and descending melodic minor).

There are three diminished triads in minor scales: ii° (natural minor, harmonic minor and descending melodic minor); vi° (ascending melodic minor); and vii° (harmonic minor and ascending melodic minor).

There is one augmented triad in minor scales: III+ (harmonic minor and ascending melodic minor).

The triads in the minor scales can be written in root position, first inversion, or second inversion. The quality of a triad (M, m, A, or d) is not affected by which note is in the bass.

When writing first-inversion or second-inversion triads in a key, be sure to spell the correct root-third-fifth first, then put the correct pitch in the bass.

Drill: Using the minor keys in the circle of fifths, spell the i, iv, and V chords (ascending and descending) in each key in root position. (a, e, b, f#, c#, g#, d#, a#, d, g, c, f, b♭, e♭, and a♭). A minor: i is A-C-E/E-C-A; iv is D-F-A/A-F-D; V is E-G#-B/B-G#-E, and so on. Be careful to raise the seventh scale degree (the third of the V): V is a major triad because it contains the leading tone (raised $\hat{7}$).

Drill: Using the minor keys in the circle of fifths, spell the i⁶, iv⁶ and V⁶ chords (ascending and descending) in each key in close position. (a, e, b, f#, c#, g#, d#, a#, d, g, c, f, b♭, e♭, and a♭). A minor: i⁶ is C-E-A/A-E-C, iv⁶ is F-A-D/D-A-F, V⁶ is G#-B-E/E-B-G#, and so on. Be careful to raise the seventh scale degree (the third of the V): V is a major triad because it contains the leading tone (raised $\hat{7}$).

Homework Assignments #10, #11, and #12, pp. 214-216

8.   Identifying Triads in Keys

To identify a triad in a key, find its root and determine the scale degree of that note.

Given:

d: _____

Answer: VI⁶

Process: Stacked in thirds: B♭-D-F; therefore, this is a first-inversion triad;
B♭ to F is a perfect fifth; therefore, this is either a major or minor triad;
B♭ is the submediant of D minor, and B♭ to D is a major third; therefore, this is the VI⁶.

Homework Assignment #13, p. 217

To identify a triad in open position in a key, find its root and determine the scale degree of that pitch. Be sure to notate the position (root, first inversion, or second inversion) when you write the roman numeral.

Given:

Eb: _____

Answer: vii°⁶

Process: Stacked in thirds: D-F-A♭; this is a 6 chord because F is the lowest note;
                    D to A♭ is a diminished fifth, so this is a diminished triad;
                    the only diminished triad in a major key is vii°, and D is $\hat{7}$ in E♭ major.

Homework Assignment #14, p. 218

PRACTICE QUIZ ON CHAPTER SIX, p. 219

Name: _____

Time limit: 15 minutes

Identify the following root-position triads as to type: major (M), minor (m), augmented (A), or diminished (d).

Example: Given:

_____

Answer: ___M___

Process: F to A is a major third
F to C is a perfect fifth

HW 1-5 only

1. _____   2. _____   3. _____   4. _____   5. _____

6. _____   7. _____   8. _____   9. _____   10. _____

11. _____   12. _____   13. _____   14. _____   15. _____

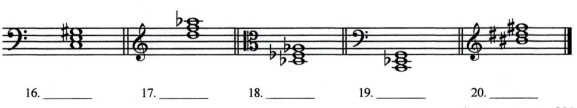

16. _____   17. _____   18. _____   19. _____   20. _____

Answers on page 221

Name: _____

Build the requested triads in the given clefs. The given note is labeled as either the root (R), third (3), or fifth (5) of the triad.

Example: Given:    Answer: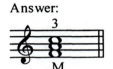

Process: Add some kind of F below and some kind of C above; F to A is a major third; F to C is a perfect fifth.

Answers on page 222

Name: _____   Time limit: 10 minutes

Identify the given root-position triad as to type (M, m, d, or A) and rewrite it in two different open
spacings. Be sure to keep the root in the bass.

Example: Given: Answer:

_____   __m__

1._____   2._____

3._____   4._____

5._____   6._____

Answers on page 223

Name: _____   Time limit: 10 minutes

Identify the given first-inversion triad as to type (M, m, d, or A) and rewrite it in two different open spacings. Be sure to keep the third of the triad in the bass.

Example: Given: Answer:

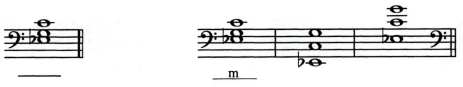

_____   __m__

1._____   2._____

3._____   4._____

5._____   6._____

Answers on page 224

Name: _____   Time limit: 10 minutes

Identify the given triad as to type (M, m, d, or A) and position (root (R), first inversion (6), or second inversion ($^6_4$)). Rewrite each triad in two different open spacings. Be sure to keep the correct note (R, 3, or 5) in the bass.

Example: Given: Answer:

_____   <u> M, 6 </u>

1._____   2._____

3._____   4._____

5._____   6._____

Answers on page 225

Name: _____

Identify the following triads as to **position** (root position (R), first inversion (6), or second inversion ($\frac{6}{4}$))
and **type** (M, m, A, or d).

Example: Given:    Answer:

_____   M, 6

Process: Stacked thirds are F-A-C;
since A is in bass, this is a 6 triad;
F-A-C is a major triad.

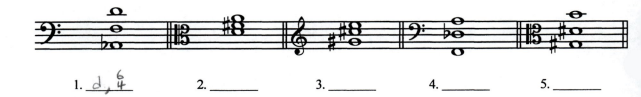

1. _d,_ $\frac{6}{4}$ 2. _____   3. _____   4. _____   5. _____

6. _____   7. _____   8. _____   9. _____   10. _____

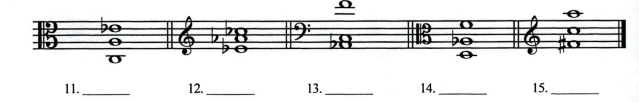

11. _____   12. _____   13. _____   14. _____   15. _____

Answers on page 226

Name: _____

Time limit: 15 minutes

Identify the following triads as to **position** (root position (R), first inversion (6), or second inversion ($\frac{6}{4}$)) and **type** (M, m, A, or d).

Example: Given:

Answer:

_____

M, 6

1. M, 6   2. _____   3. _____   4. _____   5. _____

6. _____   7. _____   8. _____   9. _____   10. _____

11. _____   12. _____   13. _____   14. _____   15. _____

16. _____   17. _____   18. _____   19. _____   20. _____

Answers on page 227

211

Name:_____   Time limit: 15 minutes

On the staff provided, build the requested root-position triads from major keys in the bass clef. Use key signatures and whole notes. Be careful to put the root as the lowest note.

Example: Given: E major, IV

                  Answer:

E: IV

                  Process: key signature is F♯-C♯-G♯-D♯
                              ∧
                              4 in E major is A
                              triad above A is A-C♯-E
                              A-C♯-E is a major triad

1. D major, V   2. E♭ major, ii   3. F♯ major, V

4. B♭ major, IV   5. G major, vii°   6. D♭ major, iii

7. B major, vi   8. A♭ major, I   9. A major, iii

10. C♭ major, vi   11. C♯ major, V   12. F major, vii°

Answers on page 228

Name: _____   Time limit: 15 minutes

On the staff provided, build the requested first- and second-inversion triads from the major scale in the **treble clef.** Use key signatures and whole notes. Be careful to place the third as the lowest pitch for first-inversion triads, and the fifth as the lowest pitch for second-inversion triads.

Example: Given: E major, IV ^{6}

Answer:

E: IV^6

Process: key signature is F#-C#-G#-D#
           $\overset{\wedge}{4}$ in E Major is A
           triad above A is A-C#-E
           A-C#-E is a major triad
           6 means first inversion, put C# on bottom

1. F major, I ^{6} 2. B major, ii $^6_4$ 3. Db major, V ^{6}

4. A major, IV ^{6} 5. Bb major, vi $^6_4$ 6. F# major, iii ^{6}

7. Cb major, I ^{6} 8. D major, vii° ^{6} 9. Gb major, V ^{6}

10. C# major, vii° ^{6} 11. Ab major, iii $^6_4$ 12. G major, ii ^{6}

Answers on page 228

Name: _____   Time limit: 15 minutes

On the staff provided, build the requested root-position triads from the minor scale in the treble clef. Use key signatures and whole notes. Be careful to put the root as the lowest pitch.

Example: Given: Eb minor, V

                Answer:

                eb: V

                Process: relative major is Gb major
                           key signature is Bb-Eb-Ab-Db-Gb-Cb
                           5̂ in eb minor is Bb
                           the major triad on Bb is Bb-D-F
                           Db in key signature: D♮ needed

1. F# minor, i   2. D minor, V   3. A minor, III+

4. C minor, V   5. A# minor, iv   6. E minor, vii°

7. F minor, VI   8. C# minor, III+   9. Bb minor, iv

10. G minor, V   11. B minor, vii°   12. G# minor, ii°

Answers on page 230

Name: _____

Time limit: 15 minutes

On the staff provided, build the requested first- and second-inversion triads from the minor scales in the treble clef. Use key signatures and whole notes. Be careful to place the third as the lowest pitch for first-inversion triads, and the fifth as the lowest pitch for second-inversion triads.

Example: Given: B♭ minor, V $^6_4$

                Answer:

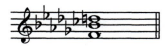

e♭:   V $^6_4$

Process: relative major is G♭ major
            key signature is B♭-E♭-A♭-D♭-G♭-C♭
            $\hat{5}$ in e♭ minor is B♭
            the major triad on B♭ is B♭-D-F
            D♭ in key signature: D♮ needed
            put fifth (F) on bottom

1. F minor, V^6 2. E minor, iv $^6_4$ 3. G minor, ii$^{\circ 6}$

4. F♯ minor, III+ ^{6} 5. B♭ minor, i^6 6. A minor, vii$^{\circ 6}$

7. C minor, iv ^{6} 8. D minor, VI $^6_4$ 9. A♭ minor, ii$^{\circ 6}$

10. C♯ minor, V ^{6} 11. D♯ minor, III $^6_4$ 12. B minor, VI ^{6}

Answers on page 231

Name: _____   Time limit: 20 minutes

On the staff provided, build the requested triads (root position, first and second inversions) from the major and minor scales in the alto clef. Use key signatures and whole notes. Be careful to place the proper pitch as the lowest note.

Example: Given: B♭ minor, vii°6

                  Answer:

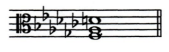

                  e♭:   vii°6

1. D major, ii 6   2. B♭ minor, V   3. E♭ major, vii° 6

4. C♯ minor, III+6   5. G major, IV $\frac{6}{4}$ 6. F♯ minor, iv

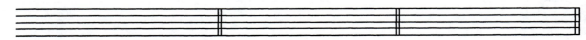

7. D♭ major, vi 6   8. E minor, iv 6   9. B major, V

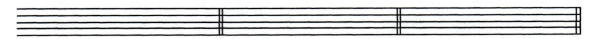

10. C minor, ii °6   11. F major, iii   12. B minor, vii° 6

13. A♭ major, I $\frac{6}{4}$ 14. F minor, V

Answers on page 232

Name: _____   Time limit: 10 minutes

Identify the given triad with the correct roman numeral and figure(s), if appropriate.

Example: Given:    Answer:

E: E:
_____   ___IV^6___

Process: pitches are C♯-A-E
                consecutive thirds are A-C♯-E;
                root is A
                A is $\hat{4}$ in E major = IV;
                C♯ is third = 6

G: c: E: A: d:
1. _____   2. _____   3. _____   4. _____   5. _____

A♭:   a: f♯:   D♭:   b:
6. _____   7. _____   8. _____   9. _____   10. _____

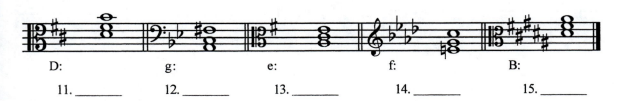

D: g: e: f: B:
11. _____   12. _____   13. _____   14. _____   15. _____

Answers on page 233

Name: _____

Time limit: 10 minutes

Identify the given triad with the correct roman numeral and figure(s), if appropriate.

Example: Given:    Answer: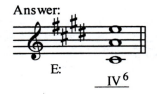

E:
_____

E:
IV^6

b: G: B♭:   f♯:   C:
1. _____   2. _____   3. _____   4. _____   5. _____

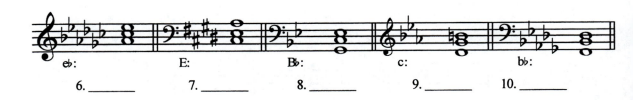

e♭:   E: B♭:   c: b♭:
6. _____   7. _____   8. _____   9. _____   10. _____

D: A♭:   c♯:   G: d:
11. _____   12. _____   13. _____   14. _____   15. _____

Answers on page 234

Name: _____

1. Identify the given triad as to type (M, m, d, or A) and position (root [R], first inversion [6], or second inversion [$^6_4$].

_____   _____   _____   _____   _____

2. Build the requested triads in the given clefs. **Use key signatures and whole notes.**

A: I^6 b: vii°^{6} B♭: I$^6_4$ f: V

D♭: V$^6_4$ e: V^6 B: IV^6 d: III^6

Answers on page 235

219

Identify the following root-position triads as to type: major (M), minor (m), augmented (A), or diminished (d).

Example: Given:

                  Answer: ___M___

                  Process: F to A is a major third
                                   F to C is a perfect fifth

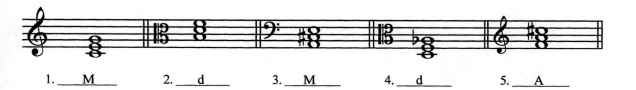

1. ___M___   2. ___d___   3. ___M___   4. ___d___   5. ___A___

6. ___d___   7. ___m___   8. ___d___   9. ___m___   10. ___A___

11. ___M___   12. ___M___   13. ___d___   14. ___A___   15. ___A___

16. ___A___   17. ___d___   18. ___m___   19. ___m___   20. ___d___

Build the requested triads in the given clefs. The given note is labeled as either the root (R), third (3), or fifth (5) of the triad.

Example: Given: Answer:

Process: Add some kind of F below and some
             kind of C above; F to A is a major
             third; F to C is a perfect fifth.

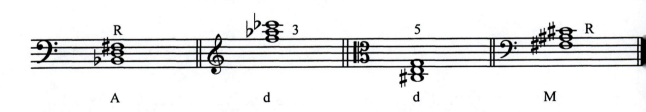

Identify the given root-position triad as to type (M, m, d, or A) and rewrite it in two different open spacings. Be sure to keep the root in the bass.

Example: Given: Answer:

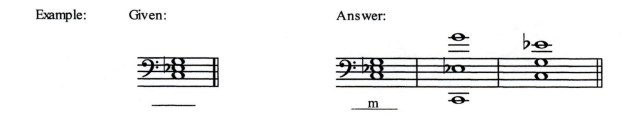

_____   ___m___

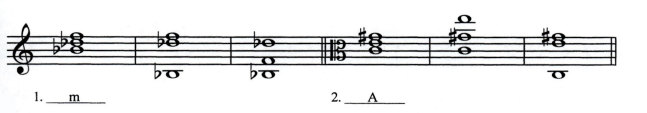

1. ___m___   2. ___A___

3. ___M___   4. ___d___

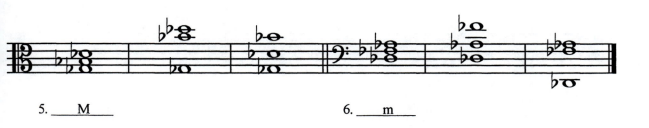

5. ___M___   6. ___m___

Identify the given first-inversion triad as to type (M, m, d, or A) and rewrite it in two different open spacings. Be sure to keep the third of the triad in the bass.

Example: Given: Answer:

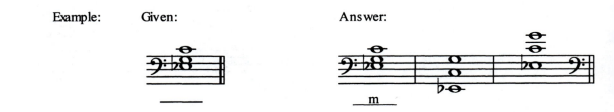

___   __m__

1. __M__   2. __m__

3. __m__   4. __A__

5. __m__   6. __d__

Identify the given triad as to type (M, m, d, or A) and position (root (R), first inversion (6), or second inversion ($\frac{6}{4}$)). Rewrite each triad in two different open spacings. Be sure to keep the correct note (R, 3, or 5) in the bass.

Example: Given: Answer:

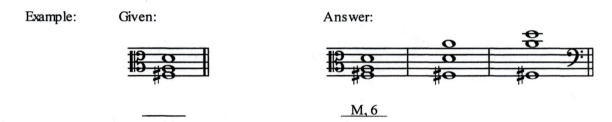

_____   M, 6

1. d, $\frac{6}{4}$ 2. m, 6

3. A, R   4. A, 6

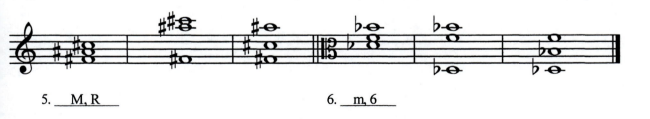

5. M, R   6. m, 6

Identify the following triads as to **position** (root position (R), first inversion (6), or second inversion ($\frac{6}{4}$)) and **type** (M, m, A, or d).

Example: Given: Answer:

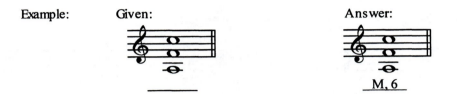

                                             M, 6

Process: Stacked thirds are F-A-C;
            since A is in bass, this is a 6 triad;
            F-A-C is a major triad.

1. __d, $\frac{6}{4}$__   2. __M, R__   3. __m, $\frac{6}{4}$__   4. __A, 6__   5. __m, R__

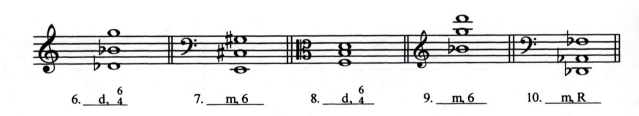

6. __d, $\frac{6}{4}$__   7. __m, 6__   8. __d, $\frac{6}{4}$__   9. __m, 6__   10. __m, R__

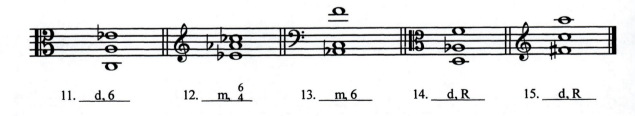

11. __d, 6__   12. __m, $\frac{6}{4}$__   13. __m, 6__   14. __d, R__   15. __d, R__

Identify the following triads as to **position** (root position (R), first inversion (6), or second inversion ($\frac{6}{4}$)) and **type** (M, m, A, or d).

Example: Given: Answer:

————   M, 6

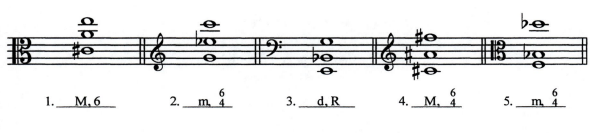

1. __M, 6__   2. __m, $\frac{6}{4}$__   3. __d, R__   4. __M, $\frac{6}{4}$__   5. __m, $\frac{6}{4}$__

6. __A, $\frac{6}{4}$__   7. __d, $\frac{6}{4}$__   8. __A, 6__   9. __m, 6__   10. __m, R__

11. __m, 6__   12. __M, $\frac{6}{4}$__   13. __A, $\frac{6}{4}$__   14. __M, $\frac{6}{4}$__   15. __M, R__

16. __m, 6__   17. __M, $\frac{6}{4}$__   18. __A, $\frac{6}{4}$__   19. __m, 6__   20. __m, $\frac{6}{4}$__

On the staff provided, build the requested root-position triads from major keys in bass clef. Use key signatures and whole notes. Be careful to put the root as the lowest pitch.

Example: Given: E major, IV

Answer:

E: IV

Process: key signature is F#-C#-G#-D#
$\hat{4}$ in E major is A
triad above A is A-C#-E
A-C#-E is a major triad

1. D major, V
D: V

2. B♭ major, ii
B♭:   ii

3. F# major, V
F#:   V

4. B♭ major, IV
B♭:   IV

5. G major, vii°
G: vii°

6. D♭ major, iii
D♭:   iii

7. B major, vi
B: vi

8. A♭ major, I
A♭:   I

9. A major, iii
A: iii

10. C♭ major, vi
C♭:   vi

11. C# major, V
C#:   V

12. F major, vii°
F: vii°

On the staff provided, build the requested first- and second-inversion triads from the major scale in the **treble clef**. Use key signatures and whole notes. Be careful to place the third as the lowest pitch for first-inversion triads, and the fifth as the lowest pitch for second-inversion triads.

Example: Given: E major, IV ^{6}

Answer:

E: IV^6

Process: key signature is F#-C#-G#-D#
           $\hat{4}$ in E Major is A
           triad above A is A-C#-E
           A-C#-E is a major triad
           6 means first inversion, put C# on bottom

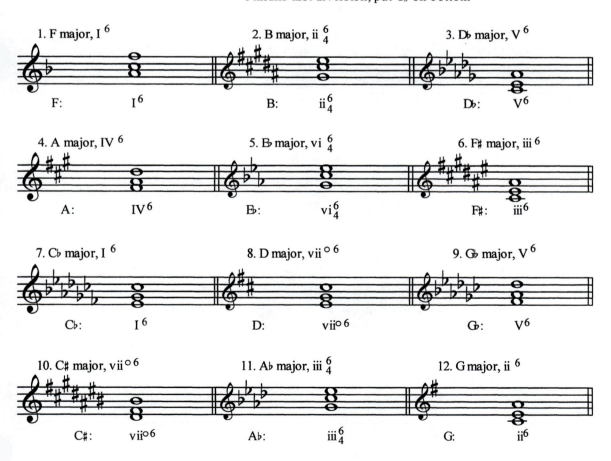

1. F major, I ^{6}

F: I^6

2. B major, ii $^6_4$

B: ii$^6_4$

3. D♭ major, V ^{6}

D♭:   V^6

4. A major, IV ^{6}

A: IV^6

5. E♭ major, vi $^6_4$

E♭:   vi$^6_4$

6. F# major, iii ^{6}

F#:   iii^6

7. C♭ major, I ^{6}

C♭:   I^6

8. D major, vii $^{\circ 6}$

D: vii$^{\circ 6}$

9. G♭ major, V ^{6}

G♭:   V^6

10. C# major, vii $^{\circ 6}$

C#:   vii$^{\circ 6}$

11. A♭ major, iii $^6_4$

A♭:   iii$^6_4$

12. G major, ii ^{6}

G: ii^6

On the staff provided, build the requested root-position triads from the minor scale in the treble clef. Use key signatures and whole notes. Be careful to put the root as the lowest pitch.

Example: Given: E♭ minor, V

Answer:

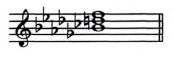

e♭:   V

Process: relative major is G♭ Major
           key signature is B♭-E♭-A♭-D♭-G♭-C♭
           $\hat{5}$ in e♭ minor is B♭
           the major triad on B♭ is B♭-D-F
           D♭ in key signature: D♮ needed

1. F♯ minor, i   2. D minor, V   3. A minor, III+

f♯:   i   d: V   a: III+

4. C minor, V   5. A♯ minor, iv   6. E minor, vii°

c: V   a♯:   iv   e: vii°

7. F minor, VI   8. C♯ minor, III+   9. B♭ minor, iv

f: VI   c♯:   III+   b♭:   iv

10. G minor, V   11. B minor, vii°   12. G♯ minor, ii°

g: V   b: vii°   g♯:   ii°

230

On the staff provided, build the requested first- and second-inversion triads from the minor scales in the treble clef. Use key signatures and whole notes. Be careful to place the third as the lowest pitch for first-inversion triads, and the fifth as the lowest pitch for second-inversion triads.

Example: Given: E♭ minor, V $^6_4$

                  Answer:

          e♭:   V $^6_4$

Process: relative major is G♭ Major
          key signature is B♭-E♭-A♭-D♭-G♭-C♭
          $\hat{5}$ in e♭ minor is B♭
          the major triad on B♭ is B♭-D-F
          D♭ in key signature: D♮ needed
          put fifth (F) on bottom

1. F minor, V ^{6} 2. E minor, iv $^6_4$ 3. G minor, ii $^{o\,6}$

  f: V^6 e: iv$^6_4$ g: ii$^{o\,6}$

4. F♯ minor, III + ^{6} 5. B♭ minor, i ^{6} 6. A minor, vii^{o6}

  f♯:   III+^{6} b♭:   i^6 a: vii^{o6}

7. C minor, iv^6 8. D minor, VI $^6_4$ 9. A♭ minor, ii$^{o\,6}$

  c: iv^6 d: VI $^6_4$ a♭:   ii^{o6}

10. C♯ minor, V ^{6} 11. D♯ minor, III $^6_4$ 12. B minor, VI ^{6}

  c♯:   V^6 d♯:   III $^6_4$ b: VI^6

231

On the staff provided, build the requested triads (root position, first and second inversions) from the major and minor scales in the alto clef. Use key signatures and whole notes. Be careful to place the proper pitch as the lowest note.

Example: Given: E♭ minor, vii°6

Answer:

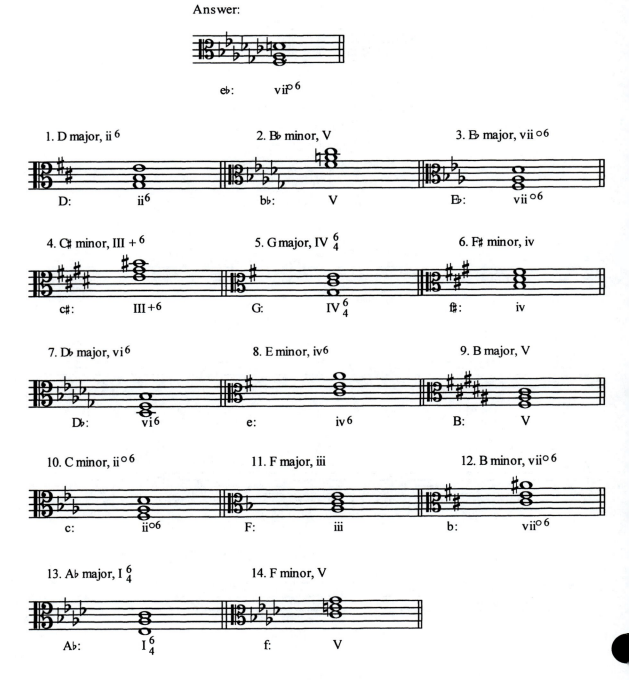

Identify the given triad with the correct roman numeral and figure(s), if appropriate.

Example: Given: Answer:

E: E:
_____   IV⁶

Process: pitches are C♯-A-E
             consecutive thirds are A-C♯-E;
             root is A
             A is $\hat{4}$ in E Major = IV;
             C♯ is third = 6

G: c: E: A: d:

1. ___IV___   2. ___i $^{6}_{4}$___   3. ___ii ⁶___   4. ___ii___   5. ___VI ⁶___

A♭:   a: f♯:   D♭:   b:

6. ___V ⁶___   7. ___ii º⁶___ 8. ___i ⁶___   9. ___vi ⁶___   10. ___V___

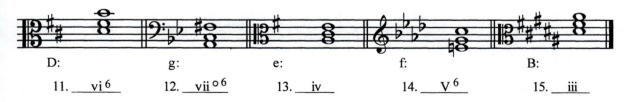

D: g: e: f: B:

11. ___vi ⁶___ 12. ___vii º⁶___ 13. ___iv___   14. ___V ⁶___   15. ___iii___

Identify the given triad with the correct roman numeral and figure(s), if appropriate.

Example: Given: Answer:

E: _____   E: ____ IV^6

b: G: E♭:   f♯:   C:

1. ___ ii$^\circ$ 2. ___ vi$^6_4$ 3. ___ iii^6 4. ___ vii$^{\circ 6}$ 5. ___ IV$^6_4$

e♭:   E: B♭:   c: b♭:

6. ___ iv   7. ___ IV^6 8. ___ ii$^6_4$ 9. ___ V$^6_4$ 10. ___ i$^6_4$

D: A♭:   c♯:   G: d:

11. ___ IV   12. ___ vi   13. ___ III^6 14. ___ I   15. ___ VI^6

1. Identify the given triad as to type (M, m, d, or A) and position (root [R], first inversion [6], or second inversion [$\frac{6}{4}$].

2. Build the requested triads in the given clefs. **Use key signatures and whole notes.**

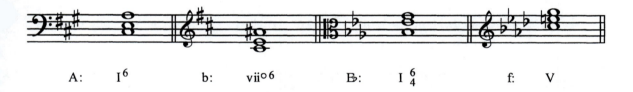

CHAPTER SIX QUIZ

NAME: _____

1. Identify the given triad as to type (M, m, d, or A) and position (root [R], first inversion [6], or second inversion [$^6_4$]. (2 points each)

_____   _____   _____   _____   _____

2. Build the requested triads in the given clefs. **Use key signatures and whole notes**. (4 points each)

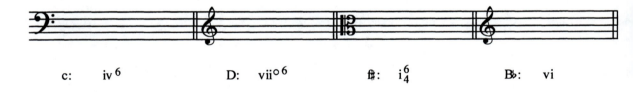

c: iv^6 D: vii^{o6} f♯:   i$^6_4$ B♭:   vi

e: ii^{o6} B: V^6 g: V^6 A♭:   iii

APPENDIX

PRACTICE FINAL EXAMS

NAME: _____

1. Provide foreground and background levels for each of the given meters. Label each example as
   simple or compound and duple, triple, or quadruple. (3 points each)

Example: Given: Answer:

$\frac{2}{4}$ _____

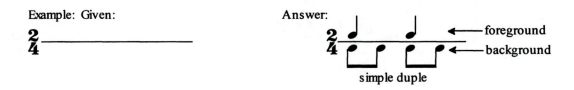
simple duple

$\frac{6}{8}$ _____

$\frac{4}{2}$ _____

2. Identify the meter of the following two examples: add a meter signature and bar lines. Examples may begin
   on a downbeat or with a pickup. (3 points each)

3. Write the requested scales in the given clefs, one octave ascending and one octave descending. (4 points each)

D♭ major

B minor, melodic

4. Fill in the blanks. (3 points each)

a.   The subtonic of A♭ minor is _____.

b.   The relative major of A# minor is _____.

c.   The supertonic of E major is _____.

d.   The subdominant of G♭ major is _____.

e.   The raised submediant of G minor is _____.

f.   The parallel minor of C# major is _____.

g.   The leading tone of F# minor is _____.

h.   The raised submediant of B♭ minor is _____.

i.   The mediant of G minor is _____.

j.   The relative major of G# minor is _____.

k.   The leading tone of C# major is _____.

l.   The mediant of E♭ major is _____.

5. Identify each of the given intervals by number **and** type.   (1 point each)

_____   _____   _____   _____

_____   _____   _____

6. Build the requested interval in the given clef, then build and identify its inversion.   (2 points each)

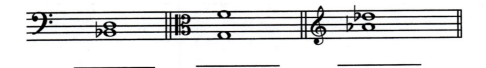

m3 ↑   _____   P5 ↓   _____   A4 ↑   _____

M7 ↓   _____   d8 ↑   _____

7. Build the requested triads in the given clefs. **Use key signatures and whole notes**. (3 points each)

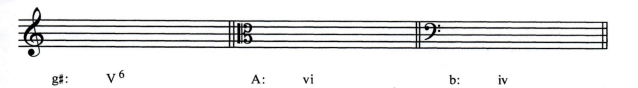

g#:   V ^{6} A: vi   b: iv

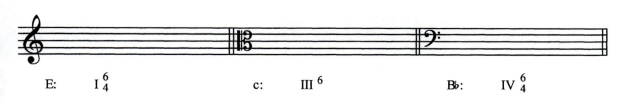

E: I $^6_4$ c: III ^{6} B♭:   IV $^6_4$

F#:   V   C♭:   ii   f: vii° ^{6}

Answers on pages 247-250

1. Provide foreground and background levels for each of the given meters. Label each example as simple or compound and duple, triple, or quadruple. (3 points each)

Example: Given: Answer:

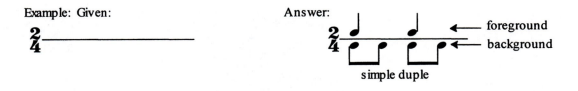

2. Identify the meter of the following two examples: add a meter signature and bar lines. Examples may begin on a downbeat or with a pickup. (3 points each)

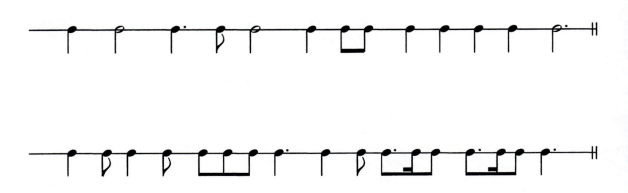

3. Write the requested scales in the given clefs, one octave ascending and one octave descending. (4 points each)

B major

F minor, melodic

4. Fill in the blanks. (3 points each)

    a.   The subtonic of E♭ minor is _____.

    b.   The relative major of B minor is _____.

    c.   The supertonic of F# major is _____.

    d.   The subdominant of C# major is _____.

    e.   The raised submediant of E minor is _____.

    f.   The parallel minor of C# major is _____.

    g.   The leading tone of G minor is _____.

    h.   The raised submediant of D minor is _____.

    i.   The mediant of C# minor is _____.

    j.   The relative major of A minor is _____.

    k.   The leading tone of A♭ major is _____.

    l.   The mediant of B major is _____.

5. Identify each of the given intervals by number **and** type.   (1 point each)

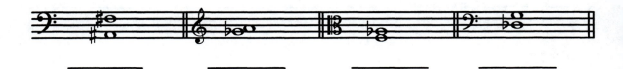

_____ _____ _____ _____

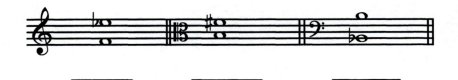

_____ _____ _____

6. Build the requested interval in the given clef, then build and identify its inversion.   (2 points each)

d7↑ _____ M2↓ _____ A1↑ _____

m3↓ _____ P5↑ _____

7. Build the requested triads in the given clefs. **Use key signatures and whole notes**. (3 points each)

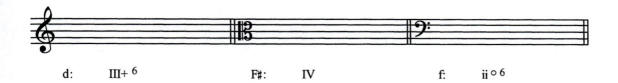

d: III+ 6   F♯:   IV   f: ii ° 6

b: i $^6_4$ D♭:   ii   A: vii °

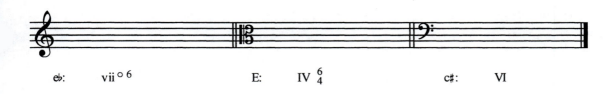

e♭:   vii ° 6   E: IV $^6_4$ c♯:   VI

Answers on pages 251-256

1. Provide foreground and background levels for each of the given meters. Label each example as simple or compound and duple, triple, or quadruple. (3 points each)

Example: Given:

$\frac{2}{4}$ ————————————

Answer:

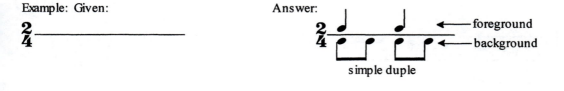

2. Identify the meter of the following two examples: add a meter signature and bar lines. Examples may begin on a downbeat or with a pickup. (3 points each)

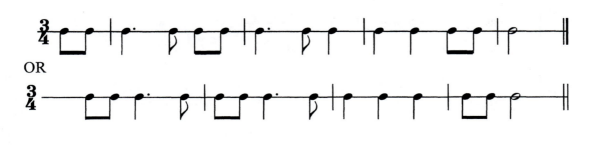

OR

3. Write the requested scales in the given clefs, one octave ascending and one octave descending.
   (4 points each)

Db major

B minor, melodic

4. Fill in the blanks. (3 points each)

    a.   The subtonic of Ab minor is ____Gb____.

    b.   The relative major of A# minor is ____C# major____.

    c.   The supertonic of E major is _____F#_____.

    d.   The subdominant of Gb major is _____Cb_____.

    e.   The raised submediant of G minor is _____E♮_____.

    f.   The parallel minor of C# major is _____C# minor_____.

    g.   The leading tone of F# minor is ____E#____.

    h.   The raised submediant of Bb minor is ____G♮____.

    i.   The mediant of G minor is ____Bb____.

    j.   The relative major of G# minor is ____B major____.

    k.   The leading tone of C# major is _____B#_____.

    l.   The mediant of Eb major is _____G_____.

5. Identify each of the given intervals by number **and** type. (1 point each)

    d5   d6   A2   A6

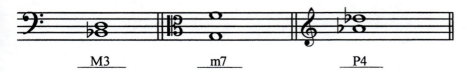

    M3   m7   P4

6. Build the requested interval in the given clef, then build and identify its inversion. (2 points each)

    m3↑   M6   P5 ↓   P4   A4↑   d5

    M7↓   m2   d8 ↑   A1

7. Build the requested triads in the given clefs. **Use key signatures and whole notes.** (3 points each)

g#:   V^6 A: vi   b: iv

E: I$^6_4$ c: III^6 Bb: IV$^6_4$

F#:   V   Cb: ii   f: vii°^{6}

1. Provide foreground and background levels for each of the given meters. Label each example as simple or compound and duple, triple, or quadruple. (3 points each)

Example: Given: Answer:

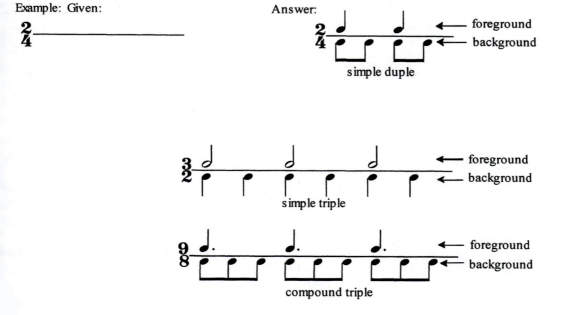

2. Identify the meter of the following two examples: add a meter signature and bar lines. Examples may begin on a downbeat or with a pickup. (3 points each)

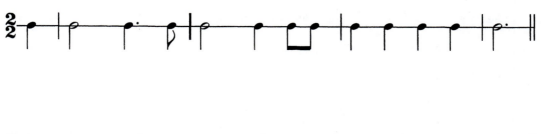

3. Write the requested scales in the given clefs, one octave ascending and one octave descending. (4 points each)

B major

F minor, melodic

4. Fill in the blanks. (3 points each)

  a. The subtonic of E♭ minor is _____D♭_____.

  b. The relative major of B minor is _____D major_____.

  c. The supertonic of F# major is _____G#_____.

  d. The subdominant of C# major is _____F#_____.

  e. The raised submediant of E minor is _____C#_____.

  f. The parallel minor of C# major is _____C# minor_____.

  g. The leading tone of G minor is _____F#_____.

  h. The raised submediant of D minor is _____B♮_____.

  i. The mediant of C# minor is _____E_____.

  j. The relative major of A minor is _____C major_____.

  k. The leading tone of A♭ major is _____G_____.

  l. The mediant of B major is _____D#_____.

5. Identify each of the given intervals by number **and** type.   (1 point each)

    m6   A2   m3   A4

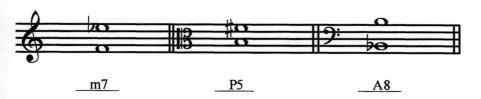

    m7   P5   A8

6. Build the requested interval in the given clef, then build and identify its inversion.   (2 points each)

    d7↑   A2   M2↓   m7   A1↑   d8

    m3↓   M6   P5↑   P4

7. Build the requested triads in the given clefs. **Use key signatures and whole notes**. (3 points each)

d: III +6   F#:   IV   f: ii o6

b: i 6/4   Db: ii   A: vii o

eb: vii o6   E: IV 6/4   c#:   VI

Index

255